CW00749661

SOUTHEND

Mull of Kintyre Reunited

SOUTHEND

Mull of Kintyre Reunited

Avril Stone

HALSGROVE

First published in Great Britain in 2009

Copyright © Avril Stone 2009

All rights reserved. No part of this publication may be reproduced,
stored in a retrieval system, or transmitted in any form or by any
means without the prior permission of the copyright holder.

British Library Cataloguing-in-Publication Data
A CIP record for this title is available from the British Library

ISBN 978 1 84114 970 7

HALSGROVE
Halsgrove House,
Ryelands Industrial Estate,
Bagley Road, Wellington, Somerset TA21 9PZ
Tel: 01823 653777   Fax: 01823 216796
email: sales@halsgrove.com

Part of the Halsgrove group of companies
Information on all Halsgrove titles is available at: www.halsgrove.com

Printed in Great Britain by CPI Antony Rowe, Wiltshire

Contents

Acknowledgements

When I agreed to write a book in the Reunited series on Southend and the Mull of Kintyre I was apprehensive about how I would be received as an 'outsider' delving into the photograph archives of many long-established families in the area. In fact I could not have wished for a better welcome. And when I requested everyone who was interested in this project to search through their albums, old boxes in lofts and under beds, I was inundated with pictures, newspaper cuttings and memorabilia.

Functions in the church hall, village hotel and tearooms and meetings with local organisations and clubs soon made me aware that the title of this series of books – 'Reunited' – is so appropriate and it was a privilege to be part of the process when friends from near and far were reunited in their memories of times past.

Southend is a close-knit community. It is the last stop in a very long cul-de-sac and therefore everyone has, at some point, to rely on their friends and neighbours for help and support, something I was extremely grateful to experience.

Every effort has been made to ensure this book is interesting, informative and accurate. I apologise for any errors, mis-spelling of names or omissions.

Sincere thanks to the following (in alphabetical order) for their loan of photographs, research and information gathering:

Argyll and Bute Archive, John Bakes, Cameron & Katherine Barbour, David & Elizabeth Barbour, May Barbour, John Barthram, Catherine Black, Linda & Bill Brannigan, Marion Brown, Alan Cameron, Martha Cameron, Alistair & Anne Cousins, Alison Eynon, Bobby Ferguson, Janet Ferguson, Jim & Moira Finlayson, Martin & Janice Forrest, Elizabeth Galbraith, John Galbraith, May Galbraith, Maria Gibbons, Ray Goodman, Sheena Graham, Frances Hill, Sheena Hume, Elizabeth Hunter, Kintyre Cultural Forum, Kintyre Photography, Hector & Esther Lamont, Rae MacGregor, James MacMillan, John MacMillan, Mairi MacMillan, Willie MacMillan, Dr. John MacVicar, Alisa Martin, David MacCallum, Jenny MacArthur, Dan & Jane McCorkindale, James McCorkindale, Neil John & Jennifer MacCorkindale, Isobel McKay, Donny McLean, Donny McLean- Boathouse, Margaret McLean, Catriona McLeod, Betty McPhee, Fiona McPhee, Peter MacShannon, Susan Paterson, Bill & Margaret Penman, Ann Ralston, Archie Reid, Joanne Reid, Belle Robertson, Alison Ronald, Inez Ronald, Lesley Ronald, Neil & Jen Ronald, Sandy Ronald, Roger & Fiona Rowland, Margaret Russell, Rev. John Russell, Nettie Semple, David Soudan, Elizabeth Souden, Donald & Eve Taylor, Dunnie Watson and Josephine Wilson.

Special thanks to my dear friend Jean Woodhams, who gently 'marks' my work with her red 'subbing' pen! Also, thanks to the Rev. Martin Forrest for making sure I spelt names correctly.

Last, but most importantly, thanks to my husband Eric and close friends for their help, patience and encouragement.

Dedication

Martin Forrest

There are times when you meet people who make a lasting impression on your life. Since moving to the Mull of Kintyre I have had the fortune to find two such men who although very different in character have enriched my life with their wit, wisdom, knowledge and kindness. I am grateful that our paths through life came together for a while in Kintyre and dedicate this book to the memory of George Gallagher and the life of Martin Forrest.

George Gallagher 1927-2009.

Introduction

View of Southend's coastline – Sanda Island and Ailsa Craig in the far distance.

Southend village lies at the southernmost tip – the Mull – of the Kintyre peninsula which is on the far western side of mainland Scotland.

From the hilltops of Southend when the weather is fine and clear you can see a ferry leave Larne in Northern Ireland and watch its passage to Stranraer on Scotland's Galloway peninsula. Or view another as it sails past Ailsa Craig, famous for its granite from which curling stones are made, then goes behind the Isle of Arran and heads for Troon on the Ayrshire coast.

Our nearest mainland is Northern Ireland just 12 miles away across the North Channel. This is a treacherous stretch of sea with strong tidal races which have caused many shipwrecks and loss of life over the centuries. But these same waters carry the Gulf Stream and provide the peninsula with a temperate climate that only rarely sees snow or frost and permits those of us who live here to boast of our own micro-climate.

The area was made world famous by Paul McCartney and his band Wings with their

One of the colony of seals that bask on the rocks off Keil Point at low tide.

haunting song "Mull of Kintyre". The lyric aptly describes the misty weather we sometimes experience, when within minutes we can be enveloped in low cloud which disappears just as quickly as it arrived.

The coastline along the western and southern edge of the Mull of Kintyre has steep, rocky cliffs where once there were several farms and hamlets, but today is moorland only inhabited by wildlife and sheep.

Southend village is sheltered from the westerly winds by the Mull. The rest of the coast has breathtakingly beautiful white sandy beaches. Rarely will you have to share these beaches with anyone other than oystercatchers and seals who swim alongside as you walk on the beach or laze on the rocks by Keil cemetery at low tide. And if you are really lucky on a warm summer's evening you could experience the spellbinding delight of watching a pod of porpoises at play as the sun goes down behind the Mull.

Twenty-first century man meets early neolithic Mull of Kintyre man. Archeologists from Bangor University and the University of Central Lancashire investigate a 6,000 year old Clyde Cairn which they have unearthed on a hilltop overlooking Southend. They found fragments of pots, flint knives and arrow heads and a jet bead which originates only from Whitby in Yorkshire.

CHAPTER 1
Before Living Memory

Kintyre has been inhabited since the Stone Age around 6000BC and historians tell us that in about 500AD the Scots from Northern Ireland crossed the 12 miles of sea to settle here. There is little doubt their first port of call would have been the shores of the Mull of Kintyre. They named this new land after their homeland Dalriada and their new country came to be known as Scotland.

St Columba's footprints carved in the top of the craggy outcrop where the saint preached to his followers.

Tradition says that in 563AD St Columba, a Christian missionary from County Donegal, landed on the Mull of Kintyre with 12 followers and founded his first church on Scottish soil. On a steep mound above Keil cemetery is a footprint carved out of stone, known as 'St Columba's footprints' and it is said that here he preached to his congregation. Every June a Conventicle (a religious service) is held at the footprints to commemorate his arrival.

From the site of the old church dedicated to St Columba at Keil, you look across a beautiful sandy bay to Dunaverty Rock with its steeply rounded headland where there once stood a fortress. This was the stronghold of the MacDonald clan who dominated the area with great force until in 1647

St Columba's Well cut out of the rock face and collecting water from the hillside.

The beautiful curved Dunaverty Bay with its white sandy beach looking towards Dunaverty Rock.

the government in Edinburgh sent an army under the command of General Leslie and the Marquis of Argyll to suppress them. After a fierce battle at Rhunahaorine on the west coast of Kintyre the 300 or so MacDonalds who had not already managed to escape to Islay or Ireland retreated to the fort at Dunaverty.

Although the River Con runs out to sea just below Dunaverty Rock the government forces managed to isolate the garrison. Without food, water or hope of help, as the MacDonalds tried to flee they were massacred by the waiting troops. A memorial stands in a field above Dunaverty Beach to those who perished on that summer's day.

Between 1647 and 1666 a great plague swept through Kintyre and many people died or left the area and it is said that the land was desolated until eventually those who had survived, or who returned, took back their property and land.

The name of the parish of Southend is a correct geographical description as it is the southernmost point of the Kintyre promontory. Until the mid seventeenth century it consisted of two parishes - Kilcolmcille (the church of Columba) where the ruins of St Columba's chapel remain, and Kilblaan where a church dedicated to St Blaan was built.

After the Reformation the two parishes were amalgamated and renamed Southend by Elizabeth, Duchess of Tollemache who was the mother of Duke John of Argyll and although, as I said, this is an accurate compass description I still feel the Duchess could have used a little more imagination and flair when naming this peninsula parish which is the jewel in the crown of the Kintyre coastline.

Being surrounded by the Atlantic Ocean it is obvious that the Mull of Kintyre's maritime history is significant and there are many tales of shipwrecks and rescues along the craggy shores of our coastline. However, the sea has never been the mainstay of this area but farming the land has.

In the mid 1700s the Duke of Argyll decided to improve his farming stock and to this end amalgamated two or more farms or smallholdings into larger units. The ousted small farmers left the country for either Ireland or the Colonies, such as Canada.

The Duke then encouraged successful farmers from Ayrshire to move into his enlarged farms here in Kintyre. This enraged the local Highland population and caused a rift for many years between them and the Lowlander's. It was only when matters of the heart overcame the matters of genealogy that the two groups of people in Southend eventually came together.

Dunaverty Rock sometimes known as the Rock of Blood as it was here in 1647 a Scottish Covenanter army held 300 MacDonald clansmen siege in their fortress on top of this headland.

In the 1950s the Duke of Argyll sold most of his Kintyre farms and other properties to his sitting tenants thereby ending the hierarchical system Southend had lived for centuries. A whole new era in both the political and social history of farming emerged.

Looking into Keil Caves where St Columba and his disciples stayed when they first arrived from Northern Ireland.

St Blaan's Church

Built at the northern edge of the village in 1774 it is the third church to stand here. The original church of Kilblaan was a few yards away on the eastern side of Conieglen Water. In 1768 when the population of the parish was 2000 and the ancient church of Kilcolmcille was too unsafe for use it was decided to build the present church at the centre of the parish and dedicate it to St Blaan who was said to be the nephew of St. Columba.

The new parish church was superior to the previous ones. The roof was Norwegian pine brought in by sea to the port of Dunaverty and for the first time there were seats for the congregation. Over a century later Ina, the Dowager Duchess of Argyll, added the porch and choir stalls and in 1911 the stained glass windows.

The Duke of Argyll was the overlord of Kintyre and chose the ministers. The first one recorded after the Reformation was the Rev. Duncan Omey who was the incumbent from 1611-1641. This system was accepted until 1794 when the then Duke appointed the Rev. Donald Campbell to the parish. However, Donald, a bachelor, was deemed by the congregation to neglect his ministerial duties and be too fond of dinner parties and social functions, and to behave in a way unbecoming to a man of the cloth! So the parishioners decided to build another church and choose their own minister.

St Columba's Church

The Relief Church of Southend was built in 1797 in the area of the village known as Muneroy. However, a dispute took place between the Gaelic-speaking Highlanders who wanted a Gaelic-speaking minister and the Lowlanders who wanted one who was English speaking. Eventually the English speaking Rev. Alexander Laing was appointed in 1799. The Highlanders returned to St Blaan's Parish Church where the Duke of Argyll continued to choose their ministers until the Disruption in 1843, after which the congregation chose their own. St Columba's Church was rebuilt in 1890 and later became part of the present Church of Scotland and joint services were held by the two churches. The redundant St Columba's Church closed in 1965.

The interior of St Columba's Church dressed for a wedding.

The Rev. Andrew McLaren Young and his wife Margaret Hendrie Young with their family outside the Manse of St Columba's Church. The Rev. Young was the minister here from 1874-1913.

Frances Young, one of the minister's daughters, was headmistress of Glenbreckerie Primary School which catered for children living on the western side of Southend. Another daughter, Isobel, became a missionary in India.

Keil Mansion House

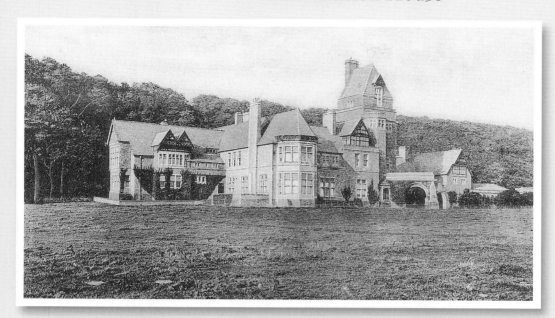

This house was built by James Nicol Fleming, a Glasgow merchant who made his fortune during the American Civil War. A smaller Keil House had stood on this land, although further back from the sea. Records going back to 1611 show that Duncan Omey minister of Kilcolmkill Church, lived there.

Then it was the home of the Omey family until 1819 when it was sold to Dr Colin McLarty of Jamaica who was at the time residing at Sanda House (Macharioch House).

It is interesting to note that at this time there were only seven landowners in Southend - the Duke of Argyll, William MacDonald of Ballyshear, John McMillan McNeil of Caskey, Donald McMillan of Lephenstrath, George McNeill of Ugadale and William McDonald of Sanda.

When Fleming acquired Keil House in 1865 he was a director of the City of Glasgow Bank. Dissatisfied with the house as it was he commissioned Campbell Douglass, a Glasgow architect, to design a mansion which befitted his financial status. Finished in 1870 it was one of the finest residences in the Western Highlands.

However, Fleming's funds were exhausted by his ambitious project and he had to borrow heavily from his bank. Unfortunately the other directors were also unscrupulous in their dealings and in October 1878 the bank crashed leaving shareholders with five million pounds of debts. Fleming fled to Spain but he eventually returned to stand trial and got a prison sentence.

After years of standing empty the property was sold in 1883 to another Glasgow merchant, Ninian Bannatyne Stewart who further improved it. Following the deaths of Mr and Mrs Stewart the house was sold to the trustees of the MacKinnon MacNeill Trust and became the Kintyre Technical College, which we refer to later.

I thank James Barbour of Machribeg for the use of his research into the history of Keil House.

The rear of Keil House with its magnificent walled kitchen gardens.

One of the ornate parlours with Romanesque pillars and plasterwork ceilings.

The entrance hall with its galleried first floor.

Ninian Bannatyne Stewart's yacht. Although this photograph was not taken at Southend it was a frequent visitor to the area.
This and the preceding four photographs, taken at the time of the Stewart's ownership, were in an album purchased at a sale in Wymess and given to the owners of Keil Farm many years later.

Another large residence at this time was Carskiey Mansion House the estate home of the McNeills for centuries who at the time of the Dunaverty massacre were on the side of the besieged MacDonalds. This picture is of the house is prior to 1904 when it was rebuilt on a much grander scale.

The Barbour Family of Aucharua

John Barbour originally moved to Aucharua Farm from West Kilbride before his marriage on 24 November, 1871 to Margaret Gemmell of Dalrioch. In a report in the Campbeltown Courier to mark the couple's 50th wedding anniversary in 1921 the Rev. Angus MacVicar said that Mr Barbour was the best type of Lowland tenant farmer – hard working, industrious, enterprising and capable. Perhaps this is why the Duke of Argyll had encouraged farmers from Ayrshire to take over his farms in Kintyre more than a century before.

John and Margaret Barbour not only had a successful and productive farm but followed this through to their own family life with 12 children – eight sons and four daughters – as seen in the photograph taken in 1897.

Back row L-R: 1) Sibella Hendrie who married Capt. James Taylor of Machrimore Farm and later the Keil Hotel. 2) John (Jack) who became a solicitor. 3) Elizabeth Wilson became a farmer's wife at Macharioch Farm. 4) James - farmer at Machribeg Farm. 5) Thomas Gemmell-farmer at High Catterdale. Middle Row:- 6) David carried on the family farm at Aucharua. 7) Margaret married John Cameron from Gartvaigh Farm. Mr John

Barbour and Mrs Margaret Barbour 8) Archibald became a Customs Officer. Front Row:- 9) Robert became a farmer at Dunglass. 10) William became a teacher. 11) Agnes Jane married Hugh Galbraith and lived at Coledrain Farm. 12) Mathew Hendrie farmed at Dalrioch.

Only three of the Barbour children did not remain in the farming world and eight of the other nine stayed in Southend. It was only Mathew that moved back to his mother's birthplace of Dalrioch in Ayrshire. And there is still a young Barbour family at Aucharua today with David Barbour the great-grandson of the original John Barbour.

The MacKay family of Lephenstrath Farm at the turn of the twentieth century.

The headmaster and primary teacher Miss Blackstock with the pupils of Southend Primary School circa 1900.

Another Ayrshire family was Archie Reid's, who farmed until recently at Keprigan Farm. Here we see Archie's grandparents John and Maryann McCrea circ. 1900. John can trace his family in the Southend area back to 1692 when they lived at Killdavie Farm and later Chiskan Farm.

Dunaverty Golf Club

On 19 April 2009 the Dunaverty Golf Course which verges on Dunaverty Beach, was 110 years old. It was on 19 March 1889 that ten sporting men met in the Argyll Arms Hotel in Campbeltown and formed the club. The first match was played on 20 April 1889. With only a month to prepare a course one surmises that the greens were not in the tip top condition that golfers enjoy today.

In the first year the club had 42 members. There was no clubhouse until a wood and corrugated iron building was erected in 1893 at the cost of £30 on the same site as today's clubhouse. Previously the members used the Argyll Arms Hotel in Southend as their watering hole!

It was not always an easy course to go around as part of it along the Brunerican shoreline was used by the Territorial Army as a rifle range, so if the warning flag was flying play had to be restricted to the holes well away from the target area.

1890 the four golfers are L-R Dick Gillon, part-time lighthouse keeper James Watson, Southend's postmaster Jim Greenlees and farmer John Cameron of High Machrimore.

Dunaverty Golf Club Autumn Meeting 16 September, 1898.

Back row L-R: Wright, Col. T.L. Brown, James Taylor, A.M. Greenlees, A.J. Gardiner, William Greenlees. Middle row:- L-R John Reid(Greenkeeper) Napier, C.J.N. Fleming, Dr. James Niven (Southend's G.P.) John Moffat, William Reid, W.S. Colville, David Colville, James Weir and Hugh McNeish. Front row:- L-R James Lothian, Rev. A.M.C. Tolmie, Neil McNeish, Duncan MacCallum and the Rev. G.M. Strang.

The Mull of Kintyre Lighthouse.

Lighthouse keeper from 1904 to 1907 Murdo Sutherland and his wife Jessie. Their grandson Hector Lamont was the last keeper at the lighthouse.

It was in 1788 that the first lighthouse was built on a cliff-top 240ft above the roaring tidal races that batter the end of the Mull of Kintyre. It is only accessible by a seven mile narrow road built over boggy land, which reaches the highest point of the Mull then zig-zags down to the lighthouse. One of its building engineers was Robert Stevenson, a close relation of the author Robert Louis Stevenson.

Due to the difficult terrain it took 22 months to build as all the materials had to be landed at Southend and then taken by horse over the mountainous road to the site. Each journey took a day. In 1817 the lighthouse keeper was awarded an extra £5 annually to enable him to keep a horse which was necessary to carry his stores from Southend.

In 1821 and again in 1830 the lighthouse was rebuilt. A foghorn was erected in 1876. The lighthouse was automated in 1996.

CHAPTER 2

1900s

Macharioch House is on the easterly edge of the Kintyre peninsula and sits at the furthest point of a circular road that starts and ends at Mill Park. Over 200 years ago the house was part of an estate owned by the MacDonalds of Sanda Island.

It was purchased by Donald MacDonald from North Uist, who renamed the house

Ballyshear. It was then sold in 1844 and again, a few years later, to the eighth Duke of Argyll who gave it to his son and heir the Marquess of Lorne on his marriage to Queen Victoria's fourth daughter Princess Louise on the 21 March, 1871.

It is doubtful that the couple spent much time at the Macharioch Estate as although Princess Louise loved the Duke of Argyll's castle at Inveraray the couple spent most of their time in London. However, Princess Louise did have a fuchsia walk planted from Macharioch House down to the sea-shore where it can still be found today.

After the death of the eighth Duke his widow Ina Dowager Duchess of Argyll, came to live at Macharioch. She became a substantial benefactor to Southend and took a great deal of interest in the village and its people and they seemingly held her in high esteem and respect.

Especially so the children when we learn from the Southend School log book dated 29 January, 1904, 'On Tuesday the Dowager Duchess of Argyll gave her annual treat to the children of the Parish. School children had a holiday.'

On 29 August 1911 it reads 'Tomorrow is a holiday, Her Grace, the Dowager Duchess of Argyll entertains the children at Macharioch House'.

She also not only improved the church building but also provided a new church hall.

The new John R. Ker *lifeboat being launched whilst its sails are being hoisted.*

When Ina, Dowager Duchess of Argyll moved from Inveraray Castle to Macharioch she brought with her Peter MacLaren and Charlie Scott her two coachmen and Peter's sister Annie who worked in the house. Peter and Charlie are seen here in the stable yard of the house.

This is the original lifeboat house which had been in use since 1869 and housed the 25ft ten-oared *John R. Ker* donated by Robert Ker in memory of his son who drowned whilst duck shooting at Ronachan Bay on the west coast of Kintyre.

The coxswain and his family lived on the upper floor of the boathouse. Most of the rest of the crew came from Campbeltown so when there was a call-out and before the boat could be launched the crew had to travel 10 miles from the town. Today it is a privately owned house.

The crowds gathered for the opening of the Dunaverty Lifeboat Station in 1904.

Argyll and Sutherland Highlanders

Southend has always had great pride in the Argyll and Sutherland Highlanders and many local young men joined the regiment and others became territorials.

Argyll and Sutherland Highlanders Tug o' War Team 1912. All these men were from Southend:- Back row L-R:- Sgt. J. Taylor, Pte. P. McMurchy, Pte. T. Gillespie, Cpl. J. Cameron. Front row:- Pte. J. McMurchy, Pte. D. Barbour, Col.Sgt. A. Scott (Team Captain) Pte. E. MacDonald and Cpl. H. Barbour.

8th Batt. (Princess Louise) Argyll &
Sutherland Highlanders – Southend,
Kintyre Section on Active Service –
April 1915.

Dugald McCallum was the blacksmith in
Southend but is seen here in his Argyll &
Sutherland Highlander's uniform.

Captain James Taylor who was tenant
farmer of Low Machrimore Farm was
commissioned in the Argyll &Sutherland
Highlanders in 1915 and served in the 8th
Battalion as a Transport Officer in France in
WWI. On his return he helped build the
airfield at Scampton in Lincolnshire.

This photo taken in 1910 shows three of Capt. James and Mrs Sibella
Taylor's daughters (Sibella was the eldest daughter of the Barbours of
Aucharua as mentioned in Chapter One) on the left: Jean Smith, who
qualified as a doctor at Glasgow University, served in India in WWII
with the Medical Corp. after which she worked in Epsom and Exeter
until she retired to Macharioch House where she died in 1990.

Margaret Gemmell (Peggy) who became a teacher and after living in
Rhodesia returned to Southend where she taught at the Primary School.
She also died in 1990.

On the right is Sibella Hendrie (Sybil) who with her youngest sister
Mary ran the Keil Hotel which their father Capt. Taylor had built for
them.

View of Dunaverty Bay, Sanda and Sheep Islands c.1920. Note the few tents above the beach where today there are many caravans.

John Cameron, who came from a long-line of Kintyre seafarers, in his WWI Naval uniform.

The Argyll Estates gamekeeper's cottage (now Waterside Cottage). Seen at the cottage door is gamekeeper Donald McLean, his wife Helen and daughter Margaret who later married Hamish Taylor son of the previously mentioned Capt. James Taylor.

Agnes Jane Barbour from Acharua Farm, 1918.

The Hunter family of Machribeg Farm 1905

The Hunter family were Ayrshire farmers who arrived in Southend in 1853 where they farmed at Machrimore then moved to Machribeg in 1862. Seated L-R: Margaret, Mrs Jeanie Hunter with James on her knee, Mr John Allan Hunter and John beside him. Behind stand William and an unknown person who may be a nursemaid.

John and Mary Armour with their family at Kilmashenachan Farm 1912 Back row:- Jean, James (who was killed in WWI) Archie and John. Front: John and Mary with son Donald between them and William beside his mother.

Agnes married Hugh Galbraith of Machrimore Mill Farm in 1920 and they moved into Coledrain Farm where their grandson Hugh Galbraith and his sons still farm today.

William Reid had this house built from which he ran his grocery shop until 1920 when he sold it to Alec Watson who had worked for him.

Photo c.1900 shows school children posing for the camera near the Argyll Hotel.

James Taylor, who was from a farming family at Ballybrennan Farm, served his apprenticeship as a carpenter in Scott's shipyard in Greenock . He later returned to Southend and took the tenancy of the Argyll Hotel until he died in 1897. It was from here that a regular coach service was run into Campbeltown. Later James Taylor's daughter Mary held the tenancy and continued with the coaches.

Some of the village cottages in the area that was known as Muneroy c.1920.

The cottages at the end are now the Muneroy Stores and Tearooms. The corrugated cottages on the left were where the coachmen from the Argyll Hotel lived.

An early twentieth-century photograph of Southend Primary School and the adjoining headmaster's house.

Pupils at the school in 1910
Back row L-R: J. McIntyre, J. Morton, R. Thomson, J. Ferguson, R. Ronald.
2nd row: J. Cameron, P. Galbraith, F. McMurchy, D. Armour, D. Watson.
3rd row: E. McQuire, M. McDonald, E. Caldwell, S. Balloch, M. McMurchy.
Front row: W. Wilson, G. Ferguson, J. McKerral.

CHAPTER 3

1920s

The memorial to the Southend servicemen of both World Wars which was built in 1920.

The tenth Duke of Argyll unveiling the War Memorial in 1920.

The Duke, a prolific diarist, recorded this on the day of his visit to Southend:

Unveiled the Kilblaan War Memorial at 3.00p.m.

Called about the town in the morning then changed out of my kilt into Uniform before lunch and at 1.45, taking Mr Lothian with me, I left in my motor for Mr MacVicar's manse at Kilblaan.

The Cross is about a mile from the Campbeltown side of Kilblaan and we waited till all tenants, at least 1500, had turned up and mustered at the Cross at Keprigan cross roads. Where there was a huge concourse.

After inspecting the Guard of Honour the service began and I gave an address before unveiling the names on the Cross it-self which had no covering upon it and the Union Jack merely covered the names let into the cairn.

Spoke to all the fathers and mothers and the other tenants afterwards who were in the enclosure and then motored back to the manse with Mrs MacVicar and the committee and gave a lift back to Campbeltown to a Mrs Brown and a Mrs Llewellyn.

Back to Campbeltown by 4.45pm and left for Inveraray and got home at 9.5pm exactly and found dinner over.

The Argyll & Sutherland Highland Territorial soldiers on their first parade after the end of the First World War outside St Blaan's Church.

The Southend Territorials march back into the village after the unveiling of the memorial.

Mrs Mary Gibson (née Taylor) who became the tenant of the Argyll Arms Hotel after her father's death, seen here with some of her hotel staff.

Mrs Gibson at the door of the Argyll Arms and her brother Capt. James Taylor with his family in his Model T Ford alongside.

Farming in the 1920s

Killervan Farm Stackyard
L-R: Donald McLean,
Duncan McCallum, John
Reid, George Ferguson,
Robert McSporran and
John Ferguson.

Cutting peat on the Moil (on the
moorland high up on the Mull of
Kintyre).

Thinning turnips
at Keprigan Farm.
On the left is
George Reid with
his brother John
on the right. They
were the sons of
John and Maryann
Reid seen in
Chapter One.
John emigrated to
farm in New
Zealand in 1929
when he was 28
years old.

George Reid with Polly rolling a field at Keprigan.

John Reid Snr seen here churning the butter in the courtyard of Keprigan Farm 1926.

The Duke of Kent who had sailed into Campbeltown harbour requested to take tea in a farmhouse kitchen. He is seen here arriving at Lephenstrath Farm where Mrs MacKay served him tea.

Archie MacKay farmer of Lephenstrath Farm drives his Morris Cowley to Dalrioch Farm in 1924.

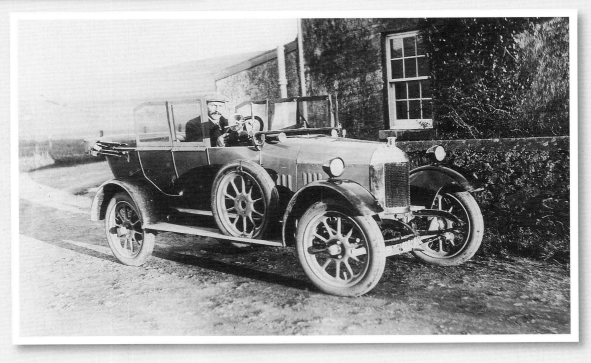

James Allan Hunter who farmed at Machribeg. His father William and mother Jane had moved to Southend from Ayrshire in 1853.

His wife Jeanie Wylie Hunter came from Knockewart in Ayrshire.

Three of the Hunter children. L-R: James (Jim) who married Margaret Taylor, Margaret (Reta) who married John Cameron and John Crawford who married Elizabeth Semple.

The wedding photograph of John Crawford Hunter and Elizabeth Semple of Carradale in 1928. They farmed at Machribeg until 1933 when they moved to Forest Lodge Farm in the village of Stock in Essex with their three children.

Fishermen

Archie and John Cameron are two brothers well remembered for their salmon and lobster fishing in Southend during the twentieth century but their family history goes further back in seafaring.

Their father Archie Cameron Snr was born on Sanda Island, one of eight children, most of whom left to live in America. Archie was a fisherman who left Sanda to work on the boats out of Campbeltown. It was here he met his future wife Margaret Ewing who came from Paisley but was visiting Campbeltown with her father a travelling salesman.

Archie Cameron Senior.

Archie and Margaret moved to Southend and lived in the cottage called Dunaverty which stands on the side of the Conieglen Water at its outlet to the sea on Brunerican Beach. Here they had three sons and three daughters.

Archie Cameron Jnr. Followed a similar path to his father. He was a fisherman and also took the supplies and post to Sanda Island and ferried the lighthouse men on and off the island. It was on one of these ferry runs that Archie met his wife to be Sarah Jane Sutherland. Sarah was a teacher and was visiting her parents on the island as her father John was the lighthouse keeper. Archie and Sarah Jane had five daughters but Sarah tragically died in childbirth.

James Cameron seen here in his Argyll & Sutherland Highlander's uniform. James died aged 23 from meningitis.

Sanda's lighthouse keeper John Sutherland with family friend Jean Budge.

Sanda Island's lighthouse and Elephant Rock.

John Cameron, Archie and Margaret's other son was a renowned salmon fisherman. He married Margaret (Reta) Brown (née Hunter) from Machribeg Farm who had been widowed in the 1914-18 War.

Reta Hunter. After her marriage to John Cameron they moved to High Machrimore where they farmed until their retirement. Reta was a successful breeder of chickens and John liked nothing better than a day at his salmon fishing. Reta and John had one daughter Sheena who later married farmer Donald Graham.

On the 17th Green of Dunaverty Golf Course on the left is Alexander Banks, the English Master at Campbeltown Grammar School and on the right is fisherman Archie Cameron whose cottage is seen in the background.

Keil School

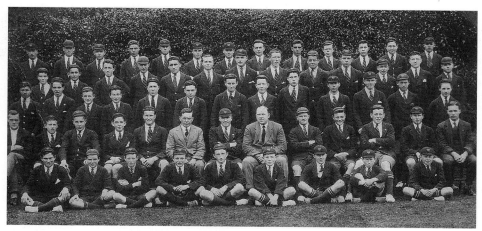

Pupils and masters of the Keil Technical School 1924

Following on from the story of Keil Mansion House in Chapter One we find that due to the generosity of entrepreneur Sir William MacKinnon, who made his fortune in commerce, finance and shipping, the Keil House was purchased and opened as Kintyre Technical School in 1915.

Sir William was born at 23 Argyll Street, Campbeltown in 1823, the son of an excise officer. After leaving the Grammar School he opened a shop in the town but soon graduated to Glasgow and entered the shipping business. By the time he was 24 he was on his way to India and a life-time of trading between Glasgow – Manchester – Calcutta and Australia.

William MacKinnon never forgot his native roots and believing that the talent of many young boys in Argyll and other crofting communities went unrecognized his great wish was to set up a wider and further educational system and enable them to have a better chance in life.

It was through his endeavours, along with his nephew Duncan MacNeill who shared in his uncle's aspirations, that the Trustees of the MacKinnon – MacNeil Fund eventually realized the two men's dreams. Unfortunately both died before the school was opened.

On 29 November 1915 there were 18 boys and two masters to start the new school. One pupil was from Southend, five from Campbeltown and the other 12 from other areas of Kintyre and the islands of Arran, Gigha, Islay and Jura.

The school ran a three year course and by 1917 there were 53 pupils. The regime was strict and austere with the boys carrying out all the domestic duties except the cooking. The kitchen garden was also cultivated by the boys to supply the school and the fields were sown with potatoes and oats. The curriculum included English, Mathematic, Physics, Chemistry, Engineering Drawing, History, Geography and, of course, Physical Training. Their day started at 7.00am with very little free time until lights out at 10.00pm.

It would appear that the school was extremely successful with many of the pupils gaining first class honours degrees at university and having successful careers. But, at 5.30pm on Sunday 7 December, 1924, a fire started in a ground floor wood store of the house and with the Campbeltown Fire Brigade taking an hour to arrive at the scene, no pump to draw water from the sea and a south-westerly wind, the house was destroyed within a few hours. The ruins remain today, the only salvaged part being used as Keil Farm.

The school moved to Helensee House, Dunbarton.

Part of the front of the building after the ravages of the fire on the night of 7 December, 1924.

The rear of the building.

Pupils of Glenbreckerie School 1925

Back row L-R: Mary Mathieson, Jean Ronald, Hugh McCorkindale, Donald McInnes, David Helm, Dan Hamilton, John Hamilton, Mary Helm, Jessie Harvie. Middle row: Janet Ronald, Janet Mathieson, U/K, Rosie Hamilton, Margaret Cameron, Barbara McCorkindale, Agnes McKendrick, U/K, Mary McInnes. Front row: Campbell, Robert McInnes, Lachie McCorkindale, John Galbraith, Archie Cameron and Jimmy Harvie.

The elders and choir of Southend Parish Church join together for a photograph on the occasion of a visit from the Moderator of the General Assembly of the Church of Scotland in 1925. Back row L-R: Archd. McKeral, Archd. Cameron, Lizzie MacKay, Lizzie Cameron, Nellie McLean, Bella Kelly, John McKerral, Jim Hunter, Archd. MacKay. Middle row: Nellie McSporran, Isa, Smith, Reta Hunter, Isabel McCallum, Peggy Campbell, Ella Cameron, Maggie Kelly, Mary Ronald, Ina Barbour. Front row: John Milloy, Rev. Dr Chassels (Moderator of the General Assembly of the Church of Scotland), Mary Barbour, Rev. A.J. MacVicar, Tom Robinson.

CHAPTER 4

1930s

Between the two World Wars the Territorials of the Argyll & Sutherland Highlanders had a stronghold here in Kintyre and none more than in Southend.

Captain John Galbraith of Polliwilline Farm (seated in the centre) seen with the Southend Territorial Army machine gun team and their winning trophy.

Annie and Alex Watson in aprons outside their shop at Seaview in the village.

Alex Watson delivers groceries to the outreaches of the parish with his horse and wagon in the 1930s. Later he became motorised!

Farming in the 1930s still had very little mechanization and the only horse-power was the four-legged kind.

Farming was a hard life but in these hay-making photographs people always look as if they are having a good time. Note that the sun was shining!

Picnic whilst making hay at Lephenstrath Farm.

L-R: Nellie McSporan, Katie McMillan and Janet Ferguson in the hay-fields of Drumavoulin Farm.

Clipping sheep at Gartvaigh Farm.

Archie MacKay Snr of Lephenstrath Farm (facing the camera) gathering early potatoes with workers from Northern Ireland.

Archie MacKay Jnr taking four cartloads of hay to the lighthouse for feed for the lighthouse keeper's cattle. This task would have taken a day to complete.

The Taylor family of Low Machrimore Farm after harnessing their horses for a day's work in the fields. On the left is Sibella Taylor, her son Hamish wears the trilby hat and on the far right is his father Capt. James Taylor.

Farmers' Children

May MacKay aged four with two of her collie pups at her Dunglass Farm home.

The third generation of the Barbour family from Acharua Farm in 1936.
L-R: Annie and identical twins Janet and Maggie with their brother John who later married May MacKay from neighbouring Dunglass Farm.

The children of Captain John Galbraith of Polliwilline Farm in the mid 1930s. L-R: Andrew, Margaret, Mary, John and Hector. Hector continued farming at Polliwilline and his son John farms there today.

James and Alec Ronald, two sons of Alexander and Rose Ronald of Kilmashenachan Farm. Another son Archie emigrated to Rhodesia where he became a farmer.

The McMillan sisters Agnes, Janet and Annie.

Archie McCallum (left) moved from Campbeltown to Macharioch in 1930 to become gardener at Macharioch House. He was a teacher of Highland dancing and had his own school of dance.

Archie's two daughters Mary and Christina (always known as Teenie) are seen here at Macharioch with their goats. They followed in their father's dancing shoes and opened their own dancing school in Southend which is still remembered with much fondness by all those who attended the classes.

The MacIntyre Family of Feochaig Farm

John and Martha MacIntyre seated with their daughter Nellie between them.
Behind them L-R Polly, Mattie, Donald, Katie, Jamie and Jackie.

Rae MacGregor, whose mother was Polly MacIntyre, related to me the story of the Danish Steamer the SS *Elizabeth* that went aground on a reef off Johnston's Point which was in sight of their farm at Feochaig.

It happened on a November night in 1935 when a south-westerly gale force storm was lashing the coastline. Nellie MacIntyre, Rae's aunt, was awakened by the noise of the rain beating on the windows, and looking out she saw the ship founding on the rocks. She woke the rest of the family and her brother Jackie drove his car as close to the headland as he could and flashed his headlights to let the crew know that help was on its way.

Jackie and his brother Jamie set off for Southend (as there were no telephones in this rural area in those days) to call the coastguards. The coastguards alerted Campbeltown lifeboat which arrived at 6.00am but was unable to carry out a rescue.

In the meantime Southend Life-Saving Brigade, a volunteer service which aided the coastguards arrived at Feochaig and battled their way down to the shore where they managed to rescue three of the youngest crew members. With the aid of a breeches buoy the rest were then hauled to safety. The wet and exhausted crew were taken to Feochaig where they were provided with hot soup and dry clothing. However, as there was a majority of females in the household some of the seamen had to settle for skirts and jumpers!

The SS Elizabeth *aground on the reef below Feochaig Farmhouse 1935.*

On the left of the stage is Teenie McCallum in a Highland dance competition at the Inveraray Games in 1938.

Southend Primary School

Sitting in the schoolhouse garden.

Sitting in the garden outside the schoolhouse is Anna Cameron with Miss MacNeill who was one of the Primary School teachers in the 1930s. Miss MacNeill married Mr Robertson, a young policeman. They moved to his new posting at Port Ellen on Islay and it was here in 1946 that their son George was born. He went on to have an acclaimed political career as a union official then the M.P. for Hamilton and after many high profile political appointments finally in1999 he became the 10th Secretary General of NATO and now has the title of Lord Robertson of Port Ellen.

This photograph taken in 1936 at the back door of the schoolhouse is of John Cameron who was headmaster of Southend School from 1934 until his untimely death aged 47 in 1951. His wife Mary stands behind him and their only daughter Anna Mairi, aged two, sits on her father's knee.

I wonder what title he would have chosen if by chance his mother and father had remained in Southend!

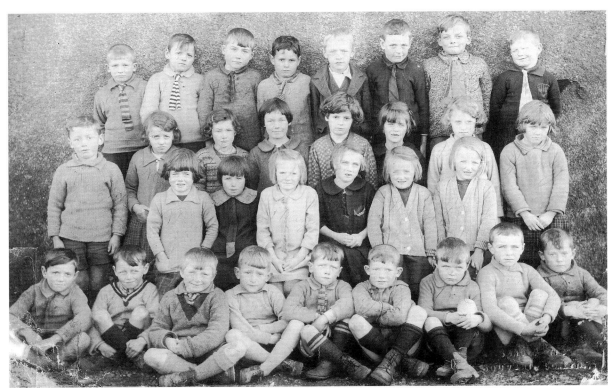

1930 Southend Primary School photograph

Back row L-R: Neil Galbraith, James Ronald, Alex Muir, Jimmy McRobbie, Kenneth MacVicar, Andrew McGuire, George McDonald, Archie McCallum. 2nd back row: Hector Galbraith, Nellie Ronald, Jean McKendrick, Isabel Jordan, Ella McRobbie, Phemmie McLachlan, Bet McConnachie, Jenny McEachran.
3rd row: Mary Muir, Margaret Jordan, Margaret Watson, Jenny Robertson, Maggie Barbour, Janet Barbour.
Front Row: Willie J. Ronald, Harvey McMillar, Neil McConnachie, Irvin Payne, James McMillan, Jack Galbraith, Neil McEachran and Hugh MacKay.

The junior pupils of Southend School 1935

Back row L-R: Robert Galbraith, John Toms, Archie McCorkindale, Annie Barbour, Ewan Stewart, John MacVicar, John Barbour. Middle row: Charlie Jordan, Gavin Muir, David Stalker, Peter Muir, Duncan Watson, Willie Young, Alex Ronald, Andrew Galbraith, Niall Taylor, Joseph Jordan, David Ronald. Front row: Agnes McMillan, Angie McMillan, Morag Blackstock, Flora McShannon, Alex Graham, James Ronald, Neil Galbraith, Margaret McMillan, Isobel Ferguson, Jessie McCallum, Minnie McLachan, Sheena Cameron, Duncan Jordan.

The Keil Hotel

In the 1930s Capt. James Taylor and his wife Sibella who farmed at Low Machrimore decided to branch out into the hotel business. James's father had been the tenant of the Argyll Arms Hotel in the village and after his death James had helped his sister Mary when she took it over. The design of the new hotel was far in advance of anything that had been built in Southend. Its elegant art deco style would be sure to attract a growing car-owning population who now took holidays further afield and off the beaten track.

But this was 1939 and World War Two was about to dash the ambitious plan.

Some of the workmen who built the hotel.

A group of painters and builders on the grass bank in front of the completed hotel.

Capt. James Taylor at the gates of the drive to the hotel.

Mrs Sibella Taylor inspects the outside of the new hotel.

Capt. Taylor's two youngest daughters, Sybil and Mary, who ran the hotel until it was sold in the 1960s.

The Keil Hotel. The building was finished in 1939, but its life as an elegant, extravagant hotel never got off the starting blocks when at the outbreak of war in September it was requisitioned by the War Office for the use as a Naval hospital. It was to be seven years before the Taylor family had their bruised and battered building handed back to them.

CHAPTER 5

1940s

For the first five years of the 1940s Britain was at war with Germany and many of Southend's young people fought for their country in the armed forces, notably in the Argyll and Sutherland Highlanders and others with the Navy in Campbeltown and at the Royal Navy Air Station at Machrihanish. The surrounding Kintyre area saw action on the sea and in the air.

As I mentioned in the previous chapter the Keil Hotel was commandeered by the War Office for the use as a Naval hospital for the duration of the war.

Duncan Watson, known to everyone as Dunnie, lived as a young boy with his parents, Duncan and Jenny, three brothers (one of which was Dunnie's twin) and two sisters at Machribeg Cottage which is a few yards away from his present home.

It is close to the sea and, conveniently for this keen golfer, right next door to Dunaverty Golf Course. Dunnie's father was the club master and golf professional at Dunaverty from 1924 until he died in 1976 and I have to be impressed that on his 75th birthday he went round the course in 75!

One of Dunnie's childhood memories is of Major Parsons, of Carskiey Estate, buying the old motor lifeboat which he renamed *The Knot* and housed in the redundant lifeboat station by Dunaverty Beach. Dunnie says that every time the Major took the boat to sea he would allow the village children to ride on it whilst it sped down the lifeboat slipway and once a year he would take as many children as he could get on board for a trip round the Kintyre coastline.

Dunnie's first job was at Low Machrimore Farm but during the war years he found himself working for the Navy as a maintenance man at the Keil Hospital. There were three surgeons stationed at the hospital and many nurses.

Dunnie explained to me that his job was to keep the boilers working and the batteries topped up. However, one evening at the end of the war when most of the staff had gone into Campbeltown for a celebration dance an emergency appendectomy presented itself. Dunnie was called into the operating theatre, which was originally the hotel dining room, and soon his crash course in being a surgeon's assistant was in progress! I'm pleased to report that both Dunnie and the patient survived the ordeal.

In 1946 when the hotel was returned to the Taylor family Dunnie was asked to continue working there – and stayed 28 years. He was responsible for maintaining all the grounds and he said that he painted the outside of the building four times using a cradle made by the village blacksmith, Duggie McCallum.

In 1978 when the hotel was for sale he went to work for the next ten years for the Rennie family at Carskiey House.

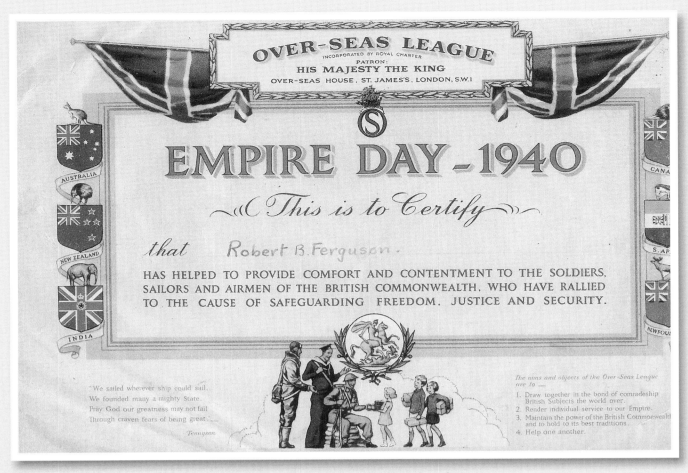

Bobby Ferguson's 1940 Empire Day Certificate

Bobby Ferguson from Kilervan Farm was a schoolboy at Southend during WWII and remembers how the children helped with the war effort by collecting sphagnum moss for making bandages (sphagnum moss has been used for centuries for its naturally occurring iodine which is noted for its antibiotic value) and also knitting scarves for the servicemen. The children would put their names on whatever they made for the servicemen who would write a thank-you letter in return.

Hugh Smith's travelling grocery van calling at Dunglass Farm on one of his weekly visits from Campbeltown. Mrs. Taggart who took rooms in the farmhouse for a month every summer is seen alighting from the van. On the left are Bet MacKinven and May MacKay waiting to do their shopping.

The five daughters of fisherman Archie Cameron and his wife Sarah Jane (known as Sally), in 1944. L-R Morag, Margaret, Jean, Cathleen and Isobel.

Dugald McCallum, the village blacksmith, seen outside his smithy at Mill Park. It is not known who the other two people are or exactly when the photograph was taken. However, there are some very clear memories of Dougie. He was born at Tangy in 1904, eldest son of the blacksmith there. The family moved to Southend when Dougie was quite young and he later carried on the family tradition by becoming Southend's blacksmith.

Dougie married Catherine McIntyre of Glenahervie Farm and they lived at the Smiddy together until Catherine died in 1974. Dougie was a football and motorcycle enthusiast and is remembered as a quiet, reserved person who was happiest in the company of the workmen who came to his Smiddy in the evenings to get their working tools and machines repaired for the next day's labours. I'm told the Smiddy was the place to be for a 'blether' of an evening whilst Dougie was working hard at his forge.

Chiskan Farm, with Bob Ralston and his wife Isabella collecting the Reid family for church.

As with the rest of the British Isles, food production intensified during the war years on Southend's farms. Sybil Taylor was no stranger to farmwork and she took over the labour in the fields of her brother Col Hamish Taylor's farm at Low Machrimore whilst he was serving in North Africa, Sicily and Italy in command of the 8th Batt. Argyll and Sutherland Highlanders.

With the war ending in 1945 the servicemen returned to their Kintyre homes and the Keil Hotel was no longer required as a hospital and was returned to the ownership of Sybil and Mary Taylor in April 1946.

Charles and Sybil Kelly after their wedding at St Blaan's Parish Church on 1st June, 1946.

Col Hamish Taylor seated 2nd left, returns to work on his farm at Low Machrimore.

The wedding guests assemble outside the Keil Hotel to celebrate not only Sybil and Charlie Kelly's marriage but also the return of the hotel which had never been used for the purpose for which it had been built.

Capt. James Taylor and his two daughters Mary and Sybil, Christmas 1946. This was their first Christmas in the hotel since it was built seven years previously.

The winter of 1947 brought the heaviest snowfall in living memory, worsened by the snow freezing, which left the roads of the Mull of Kintyre blocked and impassable for a very long time.

This led to local people having to use their initiative to clear roads, move supplies and deal with emergencies. An expectant mother who lived at Sheanachie on the Learside road went into labour and as the Campbeltown doctor could not reach the house Dr Niven from Southend walked the five miles through the snow drifts to the house, delivered the baby and then walked back again! Another woman in labour was being taken to the lifeboat station where it was planned to take her by boat to Campbeltown Hospital. But, en-route to Dunaverty Beach the baby could not wait and made his debut in a cottage on the Carskiey Estate. In other cases the lifeboat transported mums-to-be and seriously ill patients around the coast to the Campbeltown harbour. During this unusual cold spell the camera was put to good use.

From the left: Jimmy Harvey passes the time of day with Bet and Davie Barbour and Rose McConnachie on the road between Aucharua and Blasthill Farms.

The lighthouse keepers and volunteers clearing the road to the Mull of Kintyre lighthouse.

The driveway up to Killervan Farm from the main Southend road.

Clearing the road to Carskiey House and onwards to the Mull of Kintyre lighthouse.

Finding time for some fun with a snowball fight at Carskiey – in the middle is Mary McLean and on the right is John Rowe.

Waiting on Carskiey Beach for the boat to arrive with supplies from Campbeltown.

Sorting out the supplies once they had been landed at Carskiey.

On the other side of the bay, at Dunaverty, Sybil and Charlie Kelly wait with other villagers by the lifeboat station for their delivery of provisions.

Once landed the goods had to be hauled overland to their destination.

A bleak picture of the headmaster's sons Alasdair and Alan Cameron in the road outside the schoolhouse just after the great snowstorm that isolated the village.

Carskiey House

Mr and Mrs James Boyd, the owners of Carskiey House, decided to have it rebuilt and commissioned architect John Albert Rennison to design a larger and grander building. The work started in 1903 and was completed by 1909 (see Chapter 1 for photograph of the house prior to 1904). After Mrs Boyd's death her niece Mrs Parsons inherited the Carskiey Estate. While Col and Mrs Parsons lived in the mansion house their son Luke and his wife Winnifred lived at Lephenstrath House with their three children.

Major Parsons

Jenny McArthur told me that she and her brother Donald McLean lived at Ormsary Farm when they were young. Their father was one of the Duke of Argyll's gamekeepers, responsible for a large part of the Kintyre Estate. At the age of 15 Jenny left Campbeltown Grammar School to work as a children's nurse at Lephenstrath House where she helped the nanny Miss McLennand look after Luke Parson's children, Callum, Louie and Nicholas.

One of Jenny's vivid memories is of their Sunday visit to Southend Parish Church. The staff would travel together in a charabanc driven by the family chauffeur David Stewart. The Carskiey staff consisted of four gardeners, the farm manager, one byre-man, a cattleman, several shepherds, one groom, two butlers, the housekeeper, a cook and an under-cook and two housemaids.

When they arrived at the church the Major and Mrs. Parsons and their family would sit upstairs above the choir stalls and their staff would sit behind them. It was tradition in those days that each large household and farm had their own dedicated seats in the church and even today there are church-goers who can name all the pews by their original occupiers.

Jenny also recalls that on Christmas Day the estate staff with their children would gather at Carskiey House where their employers handed them all gifts after which they were allowed home for the rest of the day.

In 1948 Jenny married William McArthur and left the employ of the Carskiey Estate which was sold in the same year to Mr Appleyard from Yorkshire. The house was sold again in 1951 and then again in 1964, since when it has remained with the same family.

Lephenstrath House.

Boys Brigade Camp held at Southend School 1949.
The boys came from a deprived area of Greenock and
were led by the Rev. James L. Dow. On the left of the
photograph is headmaster John Cameron, Mr Kincaid
one of the Boys Brigade leaders and on the right is the
Rev. Angus MacVicar of Southend.

Southend School pupils 1949/50

Back row L-R: Archie McCallum, Archie Reid, Arthur Muir, Donald McShannon, Sandy Watson,
Archie Ronald and Donnie McKerral. Middle Row: John Souden, Samuel Thomson, Margaret McShannon,
Flo McMillan, Phemie Young, Sadie Millar, Elsie McPherson, Hamish Taylor and Willie McPherson.
Front row: Una Knox, Ann Leslie, Margaret Park, Isobel McMillan, Margaret Cameron, Louise
McCorkindale, Ella Millar, Mary Souden and Nessie McMillan. With headmaster Mr John Cameron
standing on the right.

CHAPTER 6

1950s

At the turn of that decade there were still the remnants of wartime austerity with many foodstuffs still rationed. However, Southend blossomed with its holiday trade. With the beautiful unspoilt countryside and white sandy beaches the desire to get away from it all made it a perfect rendezvous for weekenders, day trippers and those who could spend their entire summer holiday in the area of the Mull of Kintyre.

View of the Keil Hotel from Dunaverty Beach. Note the coaches lined up at the end of the hotel's drive.

Hamish, Ailsa and Duncan, the three children of Sybil and Charlie Kelly, who were all brought up in the hotel. Ailsa recalls how hard her mother and Aunt Mary worked for the hotel guests, many of whom would book their rooms one year to the next.

She told me the hotel was run on a strict regime with the sole purpose of pleasing the visitors. Many, in fact, became friends and she is still in contact with some of them.

Her mother and aunt were extremely good cooks and that after lunch each day they set to and her mother Sybil made the scones, shortbread and Scottish pancakes while Mary made fancy cakes for tea that was served at 4pm. People from Campbeltown would come out to the hotel just to partake in the afternoon tea.

Ailsa also recalls Marjorie Muir who worked at the hotel and what a stickler she was for polishing every piece of cutlery before placing it correctly on the dining tables. She had an amazing memory and could remember every regular visitor's requirements, such as tea, coffee, milk and sugar, from one visit to the next!

When I met Marjorie she told me of an event with the visitors that she learnt to regret. One fine hot summer's day a couple of the guests told her they did not want tea in the dining room as it was too busy so they would have tea in their bedroom. Marjorie wanting to please the very nice couple, asked if they would like her to take it up to the hotel roof (as you can see from the photographs the building had a flat roof). From then onwards, every fine day these guests would quietly disappear at tea time and Marjorie would serve them tea on the roof. However, other guests noted this couple's disappearance each day, and before long Marjorie was carrying huge trays of crockery, boiling water and cakes etc, up many flights of stairs for others who wanted this special treatment!

The Keil Hotel was also a popular choice for social functions. In 1953 Sheena Cameron of High Machrimore Farm married Donald Graham of Westback Farm, Campbeltown. They are seen here with their bridesmaid Moira McCorkindale and best man John Cameron at their reception in the hotel.

As with many Scottish towns and villages the people of the Mull of Kintyre have an inherited musical ability which not only is greatly encouraged but also enjoyed and rewarded with success.

In 1950 Southend Choir won the Rural Choir Competition at the Mod held at Dunoon. The Mod is an annual festival of Gaelic language and culture and it is held in a different town each year. Southend also won the title again in 1952 at Rothesay, at Perth in 1954 and at Largs in 1956.

In this photograph back row: Charlie Kelly, Duncan Jordan, u/k, Duncan McConnachie, Archie Ferguson, Billy McShannon, Neil McConnachie, John Barbour, Peter McKerral and Peter Muir. Second row: Elizabeth Barbour, Margaret Galbraith, Teenie McCallum, Margaret McArthur, Mary McKinnon, Sheena Cameron, Angie MacMillan, Isobel Ferguson, Helen McKerral, Miss Jackson, Annie Barbour and Nettie Cameron. Front row: Sybil Kelly, Maggie Barbour, Peggy Campbell, Margaret Cameron, Cissy Barbour, Rose McConnachie (Conductor) Mary Ronald, Bet McConnachie, May McKay and Anna Cameron.

The victorious choir at the Perth Mod in 1954

The Ladies. Back row L-R: Sybil Kelly, Maggie Barbour, Bet McConnachie, Miss Jackson, Cissie Barbour, Peggy Campbell and Margaret Cameron. Front row: May MacKay, Isobel Ferguson, Janet Barbour, Janet Ferguson, Moira McCorkindale, Helen McKerral and Nettie Cameron. The Men. Neil McConnachie, Charlie Kelly, Andrew Ronald, William McKerral, Peter McKerral, Archie Ferguson and John Barbour. The conductor is Mrs Rose MacWhirter.

Southend gets a new shop and tearoom

Work in progress on the Muneroy Cottages. In 1950 Alf and Morag Grumoli who had run the Locarno Café in Campbeltown bought the old Muneroy Cottages in the centre of Southend and had them rebuilt as the Muneroy General Stores and Tearooms.

Alf and Morag stand in the doorway of their new store when it was open for business.

View of the tearooms and garden.

Alf and Morag Grumoli's only daughter Maria with an armful of daffodils.

Southend Primary School pupils 1952

Back row L-R: Headmaster Donald McCallum, Donald MacPherson, Neil Ronald, Sandy Watson, Donnie McKerral, Archie McKerral and Infant teacher May Jackson. Middle row: Willie MacPherson, George Reid, Una McShannon, Agnes Galbraith, Samuel Thomson, Donald Taylor and Alan Cameron. Front row: Catherin Millar, Euphemia (Fay) MacMillan, Nessie MacMillan, Isobel Soudan, Janette McShannon, Helen Stalker and Elsie Ronald.

May Barbour of the Southend Scottish Women's Rural Institute presents a bouquet at the World Conference of the Institute in Edinburgh.

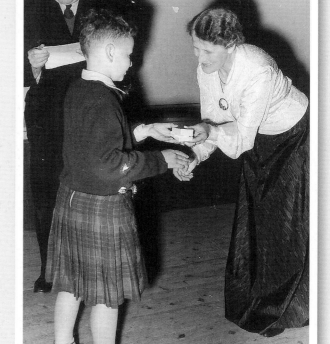

Alan Cameron receiving the Rona MacVicar medal for Gaelic singing from Mrs Blackwood, the wife of a Campbeltown Minister.

Rona MacVicar was the daughter of the Rev. Angus MacVicar who was a teacher and who sadly died shortly after winning a gold medal at the National Mod.

The MacVicar Family Story

The Rev. John and Mrs Marjorie MacVicar. This photograph was probably taken for the retirement of the minister in 1957.

In 1910 Angus John MacVicar arrived in Southend with his wife Marjorie and their two year old son, also named Angus, to become the new minister of the Church of Scotland at St Blaan's Church.

The 'Padre' as he was known to his sons - no doubt because he had served as a chaplain to the forces during WWI - came originally from North Uist. As well as serving 50 years as the clerk to the Kintyre Presbytery, in the 1950s he campaigned for Council housing to be built in Argyll and also helped establish the Auchinlee Eventide Home in Campbeltown.

In 1957 when he retired the Rev. MacVicar was the longest serving minister at St Blaan's Church and even then he never moved away from Southend as with his wife moved to the manse of the old St Columba's Church until Marjorie died in 1963 and the 'Padre' in 1970.

The MacVicar family of the Southend Manse certainly left their mark on the people of the Mull of Kintyre in the twentieth century and several of them left their mark on the world outside this far away corner of Scotland.

There were five sons and Mary Cameron, their only daughter, who always insisted on being called Rona. Rona, was born in 1917, became a teacher at Campbeltown Grammar School. Her brother John told me that she was musically gifted with a beautiful voice and only two years before her untimely death in 1949 had won the gold medal at the Glasgow Mod. She is still remembered with affection in Southend today.

Angus MacVicar, the first born son, was a renowned author of over 70 books and plays who had planned on becoming a minister like his father, but after his first failed sermon admitted that preaching was not for him. He returned to Southend and was up assistant editor of the *Campbeltown Courier* until he published his first novel (which earned him £75). Over the years he also wrote plays and documentaries for radio and television and was one of the founders of The Dunaverty Players, of which I write more later.

Angus and his wife Jean lived overlooking Dunaverty Beach until Angus died in 2001 aged 93. Their only son Jock MacVicar is a sports journalist for the *Scottish Daily Express*, specializing in golf.

Archie MacVicar was born in 1912 and became a teacher at Dunoon Grammar School. He joined the Argyll and Sutherland Highlanders when WWII broke out and was sadly killed in Sicily in 1942.

The third son was William who appears to have led a life that would befit a character from a 'Boys Own' thriller book! As a third officer on the SS *Britannia*, which was carrying 300 passengers and 100 crew from Liverpool to Bombay on 23 March 1941 off the African coast they were attacked and sunk by a German warship. All the survivors crowded into four lifeboats and William was in command of the 82 souls in the most crowded boat. His next decision would by some people be classed as madness, but instead of heading for Dakar on the Senegalese coast 600 miles away he set course for South America 1,500 miles west. William at 26 years old was an experienced seaman and knew he had more chance of reaching the American coast than he had of battling against the prevailing winds and tide to reach the nearer coastline.

William organized duties and rationing for the survivors and 23 days later they sighted the Brazilian coast. By then, alas, only 44 of the original 82 people were still alive. They were found on the beach by local fishermen who took them in canoes to a hospital at Corupu. William received the MBE for his courage and leadership. Three months after his rescue William was again at sea on the troopship SS *California* when it was bombed and sunk in the Bay of Biscay. This time he was rescued with most of his men after only a few hours in the water. He continued his wartime actions when he took part in the Normandy landings and later repatriating the British prisoners of war in Japan.

As a senior captain of the Anchor Line William MacVicar continued his lifelong career and love of the sea until his retirement in 1975. He died at home in Troon, Ayrshire in 1997.

The Rev. Kenneth MacVicar visits St Blaan's Church for the June Conventicle 1997.

L-R: Rev. Roderick McNidder, Southend's minister at the time, Rev. Charles Henderson, retired minister of the Highland Church, Campbeltown, Rev. William Bristow, retired minister who lives in Southend, Mrs Carol Paterson, Youth Worker at St Kieran's Catholic Church Campbeltown, Rev. Kenneth MacVicar, Canon Keith Pagan, Rector of St Kiaran's Scottish Episcopal Church, Campbeltown and Captain Jim Prescott of the Salvation Army, Campbeltown.

The youngest two MacVicar brothers Kenneth and John have also had distinguished careers. Kenneth was going to be a doctor but after a year at his studies volunteered for wartime duties in the RAF and after his pilot training in America and England eventually served the rest of WWII in Burma.

In peacetime he returned to St Andrew's University to study Divinity and served in the ministry from 1950 – 1990 at Kenmore Kirk in Perthshire. In 1996 he wrote about his memories of Southend, his wartime adventures and his life as a minister, in his book, *Wings of the Morning*.

Professor John MacVicar was born six years after Kenneth and 20 years after his eldest brother Angus. He remembers with affection his time at Southend school and his class of only eight pupils - Sheena Graham, Jess McCallum, Flora McShannon, Angie MacMillan, James Ronald, Neil Galbraith and his best friend John Barbour. He told me that their teacher was Miss Pattison and he recalls how all the children cried when she left the school to get married. After leaving Grammar School he graduated from Glasgow University as a doctor.

What John did not tell me was that he specialised in obstetrics and when working at the Western Infirmary and the Royal Maternity Hospital (Rotten Row) in the 1950s, along with Professor Ian Donald and Thomas Brown, he invented the ultra-sound technology for diagnosing medical conditions. This revolutionised the care of women in pregnancy and with gynaecological problems. The ultra-sound soon came into general use in scanning the unborn baby in the womb.

In 1974 John became Professor and head of the Department of Obstetrics at Leicester University Medical School where he continued his work and research in improving women's health.

As I said previously the MacVicar family of Southend Manse have certainly left their imprint on the world.

The retired minister Angus MacVicar visits the schoolhouse and headmaster's wife Mrs Morag McLeod.

Dunaverty Players

Dunaverty Players, known locally as 'The Drama', was formed in 1952 by Angus MacVicar and a group of people who were just as enthusiastic about all things theatrical. Between 1952 and 1987 Angus produced no fewer than 48 plays and in some years as many as three plays at the same time! In all, he wrote ten plays just for the Dunaverty Players, often with particular members of the company in mind. On one occasion the adjudicator of a competition they had entered commented on the successful performances of identical twins Maggie and Janet Barbour, not knowing they were really only playing themselves.

Each year the group would enter the British Drama Festival, winning their way through the local Kintyre District, Western Area, the Scottish heats and eventually on two occasions the British Finals which this small but defiantly talented group won in 1993.

These competitions had very strict rules, one of which is that they had only ten minutes from an empty stage to having everything in place. Then only five minutes from curtain down to a totally empty stage again. This procedure could make all the difference to winning or losing a competition.

Pantomimes, festival competition plays, sketches and a summer show were all staged in Dunaverty Hall and were well supported by not only local people but also visitors.

After Angus retired in 1987 his position as producer was taken by Mary Rattery, who presented another 11 magnificent productions before the 'The Drama' performed its last play in 2007 due to the closure of the Dunaverty Hall.

Cast of 'Storm Tide' performed in 1952 and 1955
Back row L-R: John McKerral, John Galbraith, Archie Ferguson, Angus MacVicar and John Barbour. Seated Janet and Maggie Barbour, Morag Grumoli, Mary Taylor and Jenny Greenlees. In front Alf Grumoli.

In 1956 the Drama Club had become so successful they decided to take their productions further afield and chartered a plane to fly them to the island of Islay to stage 'A Night of Drama'. The cast and production team are seen here boarding the plane at Campbeltown Airport.

277

Port-Ellen
Dramatic Society

presents

A Night of Drama

in the

Ramsay Memorial Hall
Port-Ellen

on Thursday, April 5, 1956
at 7.45 p.m.   Doors open at 7.15

Guest Players
Southend W.R.I. Dramatic
Club

Programme: Sixpence

The programme for the Islay production.

Morag Grumoli helps roll out the barrel when visiting one of the Islay Distilleries.

Morag once again helps a local lorry driver who has dropped his load in the road and is holding up the Dunaverty Players in the island coach.

Also in 1956 the Drama Club reached the Divisional Finals of the British Drama Competition which was being held at Greenock. This photograph was sent to me by Alan Cameron and helpfully he has given me not only the club members' names but also where they lived in Southend.

Those standing L-R: Alf Grumoli (Muneroy Stores), John Barbour (Acharua Farm), Mary Taylor (Keil Hotel), Archie Ferguson (Killervan Farm), Agnes McIntyre (Glenbreckerie School), Morag Grumoli (Muneroy), Florrie Niven (Dunaverty House), John Galbraith (Polliwilline Farm), Mrs Dow from Greenock and Producer Angus MacVicar. Seated: John McKerral (teacher from Campbeltown Grammar School), Janet Barbour Acharua Farm), Helen McKerral (Brunerican Farm), Maggie Barbour (Acharua) and Alan Cameron.

A Territorial presentation night in Campbeltown. L-R: Willie Brodie, John Barbour and Jimmy Harvey.

Husband and wife team Elsie and Alec Ronald working hard in the corn fields at Killmashenachan Farm in the early 1950s.

A group of Southend Young Farmers on a night out in Campbeltown. L-R: Donny McKerral, Donald Taylor, James McPhee, James Wilson and Neil Ronald who is known as Crocken.

The Fishermen's Tale Continues

After the sad death in childbirth of Sarah Jane Cameron, her husband Archie married Violet, who took over the role of being mother to Archie's five daughters. Violet and Archie are seen here in this atmospheric photograph taken in the Cameron home Dunaverty.

The fishermen brothers Archie and John mending their nets beside the Coniglen Water at Brunerican Beach.

Archie Cameron and Jim Russell the owner of Sanda Island seen here, towing a car on a raft from Sanda to the mainland.

There are always 'Whisky Galore' type tales around any coastline and none more so than the Mull of Kintyre peninsula. I have been told stories from past centuries of ships going aground and local men retrieving the cargo by natural means or other! Houses were soon sporting new curtains and the children went to school finely adorned in clothes made from the same bales of cloth!

Of course, these tales cannot be verified and no doubt they have a little dramatic licence about them. However, a pointer can be found in Southend School log book for 12 July 1875 which reads, 'School thinner than usual owing to the wreck of a vessel about a mile distant from school. Many of the parents with their children visiting vessel'. And on 14 July, 'Sent list of absentees to officer. The vessel is laden with oranges and lemons and the children are gathering them on the beach'.

The wreck was still proving a problem with school attendance a week later as on 18 July, 1875 the head teacher writes, 'A few of the scholars still absent from school, employed gathering firewood at the wreck, *Tantivy*'.

A report in a local newspaper of the time tells us that the schooner had left Seville in Spain with a cargo of sulphur ore and oranges and was bound for Glasgow with five crew and one passenger. The boat had gone aground on Brunerican Beach in bad weather and luckily all on board were rescued.

This photograph given to me by Ray Goodman was taken when his Grandfather Archie Cameron boarded a French trawler that had been abandoned when it was sinking in Brunerican Bay.

District Officer Ralph Rowland, on the left, with Cdr S. H. Pinchin, Inspector of the North-West Division, on board the steamer to Tobermory, during a tour and inspection of coastguard stations.

Southend Coastguard Station was the headquarters of the Coastguard Service for the West of Scotland; the only other full-time station was at Port Patrick in Galloway. Living in Southend were the District Officer, Station Officer and three coastguards and from 1953 to 1958 the District Officer was Ralph Rowland.

Ralph was a West Countryman, the son of a master butcher from Weston-Super-Mare in Somerset. When he left the Royal Marines he joined the Coastguard Service and after several postings in Devon and Cornwall was promoted and moved to the Mull of Kintyre.

As District Officer Ralph was in charge of all coastguard stations on the islands and mainland south of the Isle of Skye and would be away from home for two weeks in every month. When Ralph and his family moved to Southend his son Roger was 14 years old and attended the Grammar School before joining the Royal Navy. After his retirement Roger, his wife Margaret and daughter Fiona have returned to live in Southend.

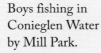

Boys fishing in Conieglen Water by Mill Park.

John Barbour attempts the High Jump at the Southend Highland Games.

The Southend Tug-O-War Team who won their competition at the Oban Games in 1958. Back Row L-R: John Barbour, Archie Ronald, Baldy MacCallum, William McKerral and Willie John Ronald. Front row: Archie Ferguson, Archie McCorkindale, Duncan MacPhee and John MacGuire.

Three Southend ladies visit the 1959 Summer Show in Campbeltown. L-R: Peggy Campbell, Isobel Galbraith and Morag McLeod with her son Murdo in front.

CHAPTER 7

1960s

The Salmon That Did Not Get Away!

Hamish Kelly proudly displays his prize catch which he later sold to his Aunt Mary at the Keil Hotel.

The Cameron brothers' family home Dunaverty sandwiched between the golf course, Brunerican Beach and Dunaverty Rock.

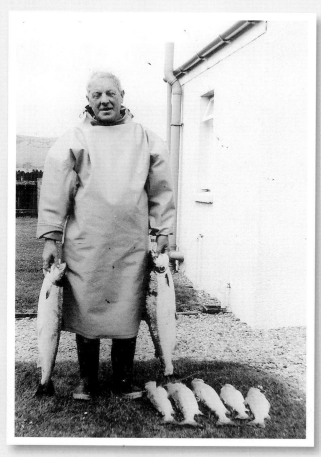

Archie Cameron lays out his catch on the lawn outside his house at Dunaverty.

Archie Cameron - this time his catch is a box of lobsters.

Dolly Armour and her sister Mary Sloan, on holiday from Glasgow, watch as John Cameron wraps a salmon in shiggens (reeds) to keep it fresh. John's daughter Sheena told me that her father would either sell his fish to the local hotels in Southend or Campbeltown or to Gilchrist the fishmongers in the town. Sheena also recalls how sometimes she delivered the salmon to the 'big' houses at High Askomil in Campbeltown and how she had to go to the staff entrance at the back with her father's catch of the day. All surplus fish would be wrapped in shiggens and sent up to Unkles, the Glasgow fishmongers.

Hughie Stewart who worked with both the Cameron brothers is out fishing here with Archie.

Hughie Stewart sitting on the boat named after John Cameron's daughter, with Kathleen Marks the daughter of Southend's minister between 1958-1971 the Rev. James Marks.

Archie Cameron pulling in one of his lobster pots.

Day Trippers

Archie takes a group of ladies for a boat trip to the island of Sanda.

John Cameron prepares to let go aft before leaving Dunaverty slipway.

Three men in a boat!

Jim Russell, the owner of Sanda Island, Archie Cameron and Andrew Galbraith on a day trip to Cushendun in Northern Ireland. (When I asked Archie Cameron's grandson Ray how he knew where the men were going he replied, "Because they're dressed in their Sunday Best"!)

Archie Cameron on the left and his brother John on the right go over to Sanda to say farewell to Jim and Jean Russell before they sell the island. John's daughter Sheena said she loved going over to Sanda as the Russells made you so welcome and Jean always had a wonderful high tea ready for your visit.

On the left, Jack Bruce from the rock group 'Cream' who bought Sanda Island from Jim and Jean Russell, seen here with Archie Cameron.

Down on the Farm

Farmer Alec Ronald takes the Girl Guides for a trip around farm whilst they were on summer camp at Kilmashenachan.

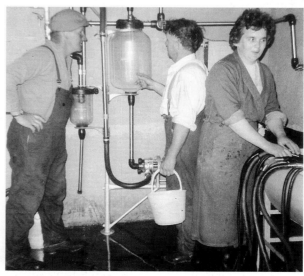

Alec Ronald with Tommy and Susan Allan in the milking parlour at Benton Farm in 1966.

Mechanization Arrives on Southend Farms

The first combine harvester in the area arrives at Low Machrimore Farm in 1962. Driving the harvester is Donald Taylor. Standing L-R: Dougie Martin (miller at Mill Park), David McKerral (Lephenstrath Farm) Col Hamish Taylor (Owner of Low Machrimore Farm), HamishTaylor (Kilblaan Farm), Peter McKerral and John Barbour of Aucharua Farm.

1 May, 1962 was the first day of bulk collection of milk for the Campbeltown Creamery. There were eight farms in the Southend area with bulk storage tanks for their milk. In this picture taken at Low Machrimore Farm the tanker is loaded while Donald Taylor, John Darroch from British Road Services, Hamish Taylor, lady U/K, man from the Milk Marketing Board and Archie Rankin the lorry driver, all line up for their photograph to be taken.

Morag Cameron gets married and is pictured with her sisters Back row L-R: Isobel, Morag and Cathleen. Sitting: Jean, their step mother Violet, father Archie and Margaret. How they have changed since their photograph in Chapter 5.

John Reid who tended the gardens of Carskiey House for many years, seen here on the garden steps in 1963.

The 1960s were a boom time for the two hotels in Southend but disaster struck at Easter 1960 when a fire destroyed the old part of the Argyll Arms Hotel. However, the owner had a new wing built in a similar style as the Keil Hotel, and it was open again by the August of the same year. Those builders certainly deserved a bonus!

The Argyll Hotel was so busy that in the summer they had to employ students from outside the area as staff. L-R Janet Lynn, Peggy Alexander and Rose Girvan, outside the caravan that some of the students would stay in. This is the summer of 1963.

On the left is Sheena Graham and her mother Reta Cameron on the right when they met Mrs Barr for afternoon tea at the Keil Hotel.

Southend Branch of the Scottish Women's Rural Institute were the winners of the shield for the most points gained over all the competitions at the Annual Argyll W.R.I. Federation Rally held at Oban in 1962.

Proudly displaying the winning shield, outside St Columba's Church in the village when they returned triumphant are, L-R: Elsie Ronald, Isobel Russell, May MacKay, Annie Alexander –President, Margaret Cameron, May MacLean, Janet Ferguson and Jeanie Reid.

A 1960s' wedding at St Blaan's Church, The bride is Annie Barbour, the groom, William Gillies, the best man is Colin Gillies and the bride's sisters were bridesmaids, on the left Janet Barbour and on the right her twin Margaret.

Headmaster of the Southend Primary School between 1958 and 1974 was Murdo McLeod. He was also the first Chairman of the Southend Community Council and instigated the building of the steps up to St Columba's footprints. When he retired from the school with Morag his wife they rescued the dilapidated cottage, 'Kilbride', which overlooks the village and the sea, and lived there the rest of their lives.

James McCorkindale, aged 8 years old, who had stepped into his mother and grandfather's Highland dancing shoes, is seen here in 1964 after winning the Scottish Championship Trophy at Cowl in 1964. James now has his own dancing school and travels the world as an instructor and examiner in Highland dance.

Colin McShannon with his mother Mary. Colin proudly holds the Carskiey Cup which was awarded to the overall winner of all the sporting events held at the Southend Games.

This is Mairi MacMillan helping out at her father's petrol station in Southend village in 1961. The car belonged to a couple who were on holiday and had driven down to Southend to spend the day. The driver got Mairi to pose for the photograph and that was the end of the story. Or so they thought. Thirty years later the driver came back and left this photograph with Angus MacVicar, who he just happened to meet by Dunaverty Beach. He told Angus the story and later that day Angus gave the picture to Mairi. Her father James MacMillan tells a similar 'deja vu' story. He told me that he was going about his business one day serving a customer with petrol and was just passing the time of day telling him that this was, after all, "God's Country", and the man replied, "I was last here 15 years ago and you told me exactly the same thing then"! Only goes to prove that James is consistent!

CHAPTER 8

1970s

The photographs for the 1970s seem to be mostly all smiles and happy occasions and none was happier than when Anne McLeod married Campbeltown's new young vet Alistair Cousins. They are pictured outside the Keil Hotel where their reception was held in October 1970

Anne's father Murdo McLeod here on the right of the picture and teacher Mrs Peggy Hunter at the back on the left. The pupils Back row L-R: Joyce Buick, Wilma Ferguson, Ian Barbour, Ian Galbraith, Peter McKerral, Jim Semple, Helen Ronald, Anne McSporran, Andrew Russell and u/k.
Middle row: Robert Ferguson, ? Cammish, Frances Galbraith, Margo McConnachie, Ellen McAllister, Jennifer Galbraith, Mary McSporran, Wilma MacMillan, Catherine Ronald, Alison Barbour, Alison MacMillan.
Front row: George MacMillan, Stephen McGuffey, David McCallum, Sally Scott, Rolline Harvey, Bobby McKerral, Archie McCallum and Callum MacMillan.

Glenbreackerie
School pupils 1971.
Back row L-R:
Teacher Mrs
McIntyre,
C. McLean,
C. Ronald, J. Reid,
K. Ronald,
D. McLean and
N. Ronald.
Front row:
J. McLean,
D. Johnstone,
A. Ronald,
C. Ronald,
I. McPherson,
J. Cameron,
J. Ronald and
W. McLean.

Glenbreackerie School as it is in 2009, disused and for sale.

Southend's young Highland dancers enter a competition at the Campbeltown Agricultural Show in 1971. L-R: Jane Cameron, Margo McConnachie, Callum MacMillan, Frances Galbraith and Alison Barbour. Playing the bagpipes behind the dancers is the Duke of Argyll's personal Piper, Pipe Major Ronald McCallum.

The sun shone and all was well with the world when Daniel and Jen Black arrived at their caravan at Dunaverty Beach after a long drive from their home at Linwood.

Also enjoying the good weather in 1971 was Archie Cameron when he took his daughter Cathleen and grandson Ray for a trip around the bay in his boat the *Wrecks*.

In June 1974 a special pageant was held to commemorate the arrival of St Columba to the shores of the Mull of Kintyre. This picture of the re-enactment which was played by local people was used on the front cover of the magazine, *Life and Work*. St Columba was played by Alistair Cousins and the little boy he is lifting is Robert Ferguson.

On the 24 June 1974 the new Sunday School Rooms commemorating the Rev. and Mrs Angus MacVicar were opened at St Blaan's Church. The Works Committee were back row L-R: John McCorkindale, J. Barbour, A. Cameron and Col Hamish Taylor. Front row: Rev. John Russell, J. Ronald, Peter McKerral, A. Barbour, J. Greenlees and R. Kelly.

Southend Brownie Pack in the School Hall in 1974.
Back row L-R: Snowy Owl Mairi MacMillan, District Commissioner Elsie Ronald, Brown Owl Catriona McLeod, Tawny Owl Jennifer McCorkindale and Guide helpers Marion Henderson and Melina MacMillan. 2nd row: Alison MacMillan, Alison Barbour, Helen Ronald, Anne McSporran and Wilma Ferguson. 3rd row: Jane Cameron, Frances Galbraith, Jennifer Cameron, Eileen McIntyre and Catherine Ronald. Front row: Sally Scott, Willma MacMillan, Mary McSporran, Rolline Harvey and Margo McConnachie.

When the new coastguard Mr Parkington and his wife were posted to Southend they started a Scout Troop which meant the boys no longer had to make the journey into Campbeltown. Back row L-R: Mr and Mrs Parkington, Kate McKerrall, Mairi MacMillan. Middle row: James McLean, Bobby McKerrall, George MacMillan. Archie McCallum. Front row: Richard Camish, David Johnston, David McKillop and Jonathon Camish.

The Dunaverty Players stage the play, 'Rise and Shine' in 1975. Back row L-R: Margaret Cameron, Maureen Johnston, Dr Alistair Maden, Hamish Buchanan and Janet Ferguson. Front row: Mabel Maden, John McKerral, James Johnston, Jean MacVicar and Jennifer McKerral.

The Project Group of the Bible Class held in The MacVicar Rooms was a continuation of the Sunday School but for teenagers. The Rev. Russell told me that one of their projects was to have a 'beach clean up' event.
The group here are back row L-R: Andrew Russell, Hugh McCorkindale, Callum MacMillan, Ian Galbraith, Rev. John Russell, Peter McKerral and Ian Barbour. Sitting: Anne McSporran, Kathleen Barbour, Wilma Ferguson, Helen Ronald, Jane Cameron, Alison MacMillan, Virgina McKenna and Alison Barbour.

A group of the James McCorkindale Dancers from Southend pose on the rocks at Macharioch Beach, L-R: Mary McSporran, Frances Galbraith, Jennifer Galbraith, Mary Wilson, Rolline Harvey, Eileen McIntyre, Lesley Galbraith and Elizabeth McPhee.

An Exhibition Golf Match at Dunaverty Golf Club between three Women Champions. L-R: Hamish Taylor with the Welsh Champion Tegwen Perkins, Dan McCorkindale with the Irish Champion Mary McKenna, Donald Taylor with Southend's own Scottish Champion Belle Robertson (née McCorkindale).

The Queen's Silver Jubilee year 1977 saw many events to commemorate the occasion. One of these certainly put the James McCorkindale Dancing School on the map when these dancers from Southend won through the Argyll then Scottish heats to win the British final held at Newcastle. Pictured here with James, who chose the music and arranged the choreography for each heat are L-R Jennifer Galbraith, Rolline Harvey, Mary McSporran and Frances Galbraith.

The cast and crew of the 1977 Dunaverty Players productions of 'Pop Goes the Patient' and 'Halloween'.

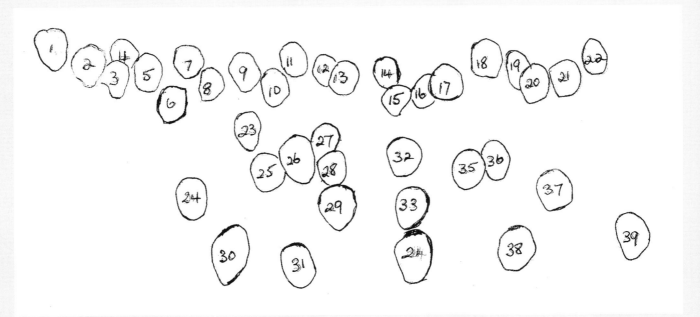

The numbered list relates to numbered outline.
1. Allan Lamont 2. Joan Coffield. 3. Jenny Strang. 4. Jock MacVicar. 5. Sybil Kelly. 6. Jean MacVicar. 7. John McKerral. 8. Jennifer McKerral. 9. Unknown. 10. Peggy Campbell. 11. Unknown. 12. Les Hutchins. 13. Jan Carruthers. 14. Jim Johnston. 15. Olive Wadsworth. 16. Mabel Maiden. 17. Janet Ferguson. 18. Bill Hunter. 19. Hamish Buchanan. 20. John Henderson. 21. Mary Taylor. 22. Angus MacVicar. 23. Maureen Johnston. 24. Barbara Lamont. 25. Mary Bowen. 26. James McCorkindale. 27. Alec Ronald. 28. Janet Barbour. 29. Rachel Bulloch. 30. Callum Semple. 31. Iain Rattray. 32. Rosemary Ronald. 33. Elspeth Craig. 34. Ronald Togneri. 35. Mhairi MacMillan. 36. Margaret Cameron. 37. Alistair Maiden. 38. Donald Kelly. 39. Parkin Raine.

St Blaan's congregation gather around the Rev. John and Mrs Russell to wish them good luck when they left Southend for Dunkeld in January, 1978.

On the right of the picture is James McCorkindale with his dancers from Southend at a Highland dancing competition. The piper is William McCallum. Back row L-R: Sheena Moffatt, Catriona McPherson, Jo-Anne Milligan, Heather McPherson, Joanne Currie and Iona Campbell. Middle row: Jennifer Galbraith, Rolline Harvey, Eileen McIntyre, Mary Wilson, Gwen Drysdale and Frances Galbraith. Front row: Carol Norquay, Elizabeth McPhee, Mary McSporran and Catherine McLean.

The Rev. William and Mrs Nelson in Southend Manse where they resided from 1978 – 1987.

Catherine McLean is the Princess of the Church Gala in 1979.

In 1979, the Dunaverty Players stage their pantomime, 'Mother Goose's Golden Christmas'.

The victorious Keil Hotel Darts Team with their trophy. Back row L-R: Terry McKenna, Marlene McKenna, Donny McLean, Alec Ronald, Archie McCorkindale and Billy Ronald. Front row: Gus McConnachie, Alistair Sowden, Duncan Watson, Charlie McPherson and Neil John McCorkindale.

The 1970s saw Dunaverty Lifeboat Station disintegrate and blow away during a spate of bad weather.

CHAPTER 9

1980s

Southend Coastguards

John MacMillan who served 36 years as an auxiliary coastguard at Southend was born at Macribeg Cottage which is stone's throw from his present address. As previously said, Southend was the H.Q. station for the West of Scotland with a District Officer-in-Charge, three full-time coastguards and at least three part-time auxiliary coastguards.

When John joined in 1959 he shared his duties with Dunnie Watson and Neil Paterson and they manned the look-out station on the hill above Pennyseorach Farm between 10pm and 7am each day and in rough weather worked 24 hours a day.

When the full-time coastguard station in Southend closed in 1976 and moved to Campbeltown, John became Officer-in-Charge of the 22 other Mull of Kintyre auxiliary coastguards. He received the MBE for his service to HM Coastguards in 1994 .

At a Coastguard Competition held at Greenock in 1984 the Southend team were the winners of the Breeches Buoy Competition. Back row L-R: Neil John McCorkindale, Duncan Watson, George McLean, Campbell Paterson, Archie McCorkindale, Alec Harvey, David Soudan, Alistair Souden, Donald McPherson and Hamish Paterson. Front row: Donny McLean, John Souden, Jake McShannon, Willie MacMillan, Duncan Watson and Officer-in-Charge John MacMillan.

The presentation at the Keil Hotel of the trophies won at the Greenock Coastguard Competition. L-R: District Controller Bob Woodwark, Coastguard in Charge of Sector Peter Willett, Campbell Paterson, Duncan Watson, Alistair Souden, George McLean, Donny McLean, Hamish Paterson, Alec Harvey, Duncan Watson Snr, Willie MacMillan, Neil John McCorkindale, Donald McPherson, John MacMillan, Dick Slaney and the Clyde Regional Controller.

Neil John McCorkindale third from the left receives his medal for 21 years with the Coastguard Service. In 2009 he will have served 40 years with the service. The two officers on the left of the picture are Peter Willett and Paul Lane. Officer-in-Charge of Southend, John MacMillan is on the right of the picture.

The Southend Coastguards in 1988. Standing L-R: George MacMillan, Hamish Paterson, Alec Harvey, Duncan Watson, Neil John McCorkindale, Alistair Souden, U/K, Campbell Paterson and Paul Lane. Middle row: George McLean, Willie MacMillan and Peter Willett. Front row: John MacMillan, John McShannon and Donnie McLean.

The lighthouse keepers on Sanda Island Eric Bruce and Hector Lamont awaiting supplies to arrive on the slipway below the lighthouse.

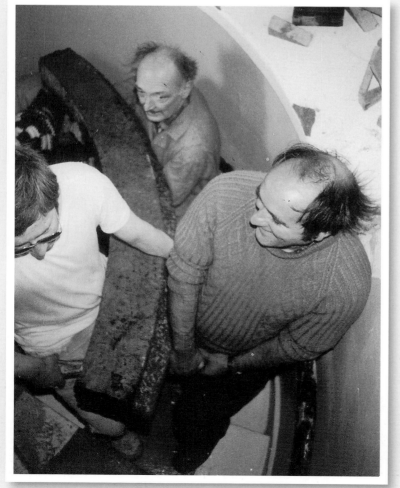

Many of the lighthouse repairs were carried out by the keepers. Hector Lamont, the keeper, gets a helping hand from Kenny Stein, in the centre, to lift a girder up the lighthouse steps. This was no job for the faint-hearted!

The Sporting 80's

The sack-race at the 1980s Southend Highland Games: Front centre is Andrew Bawn and on the right is Alistair Campbell.

John McCorkindale scrutinizing John Cameron as he takes the High Jump at the Highland Games in 1981.

Southend's Football Team in 1980
Standing L-R: Alec Ronald, Archie Ronald, John Cameron, John Galbraith, Sandy Ronald, Roderick Angus, Malcolm Ballantyne, Ian McIntyre and James McShannon. Kneeling: Donald McSporran, Hamish Paterson, Bruce McConnachie, Paul Izett, John McCormack, Alan Glendenning, Peter Paterson and Kevin MacMillan.

The trophy-winning Southend Darts Team. Back row L-R: Hamish Taylor, John Bateson, Hamish Paterson, Richard Semple, Neil John McCorkindale and Campbell Paterson. Front row: Archie Ronald, George MacMillan and John Galbraith.

Southend Primary School Shinty Team display their new strip supplied by their sponsor, the Keil Hotel. Back row L-R: Nick and Ann owners of the Keil Hotel and headmaster Martin Motherwell. Middle row: Morag McCorkindale, Justin O'Brien, Craig McInnis, Callum Semple and Tom Miller. Front row: Helen Miller, Mairi McCorkindale, David Swain, John McTaggart and Richard McKerral.

When golfing enthusiast Mrs Jean McDougall celebrated her 79th birthday in 1985 she did so in her usual way by a playing a round of golf with her friends of the Dunaverty Ladies Golf Club. As Jean tees off her friends looking on are L-R: Bet Barbour, Elsie McKinlay, Elsie Ronald, Jean MacVicar, Peggy Campbell, Martha Cameron, Cissie McConnachie, Janet Ferguson, Helen Ronald, Kate McNair, Margaret Cameron, Ester Bell, Jill Middleton and Jane McCorkindale.

Jane McCorkindale holding just two of the six trophies she was presented with at the annual prize-giving of the Dunaverty Golf Club in 1985. Jane has won the Championship Plate 19 times to date.

Well Known Characters

Two men who were well-known and frequent visitors to many homes in the Southend area were Harvey MacMillan and Cushi Mohamed.

Harvey MacMillan was born at Muneroy Cottages in Southend and like many other young men joined the Argyll and Sutherland Highlander Territorial Army and was one of the first to volunteer for duty when WWII started. Harvey was soon facing the blistering heat of the Western Desert and thankfully lived to reminisce around many a farmhouse table and the bar of the Argyll Arms about his exploits when serving with the Desert Rats. Harvey is remembered with a great deal of affection by all those who came into contact with him. He is seen here trimming the hedges around the garden of Polliwilline Farmhouse.

Cushi Mohamed unloads his case in Polliwilline Farm kitchen to show Mary Galbraith all his goods.

Cushi was a travelling salesman who would visit all the farms and outlying houses both north and south of Campbeltown. Nothing too unusual about that, you may think. However, Cushi did all his travelling by bicycle! He carried his wares, mainly clothing, in a suitcase fitted into a metal frame on the front of the bike. As the years passed and Cushi found the ten miles from Campbeltown rather a long haul he would load the bike onto the service bus to Southend and then cycle around his patch before catching the bus home in the evening.

Wonderful long sunny summer holidays when two boys could just mess about in a boat is how Ray Goodman (with the oars) can remember those halcyon days of the mid 1980s when he and his friend David Barbour would escape down to the sea.

The performance of 'The Strawberry', by The Dunaverty Players won them second place in the Best Comedy at the Argyll Drama Festival in 1985. L-R: Ralph Davidson, Jan McCorkindale, John Barbour, Barbara Lamont, Linda Brannigan, Linda Nelson, Isobel Carter and David McCallum.

Pupils of the McCorkindale School of Dancing with their awards at St Blaan's Hall in 1980. Back row L-R: Mary Wilson, U/K, Frances Galbraith, Joanne Milligan and Elizabeth McPhee. Front row: Sheena Moffat, Alison Bawn, Sheena Ronald, Anna McLaughlan and U/K.

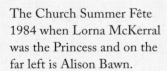

The Church Summer Fête 1984 when Lorna McKerral was the Princess and on the far left is Alison Bawn.

At Tobermory on the island of Mull, Joanne Milligan wins this magnificent trophy for her Highland dancing.

There is more success for the McCorkindale Dancers when Sheena Ronald, John Kerr and Joanne Milligan win at the British Championships at Paisley.

Southend's SWRI do some enterprising advertising with their motorised fancy dress.

The Church Gala Night on 8 August, 1984 saw an 'It's a Knockout' competition. Miss Muffet and the Spiders are L-R: Elizabeth Galbraith, Mary Cameron, Inez and Malcom Ronald, Hugh Galbraith and Thomas Cameron.

Farming News

Hugh McCorkindale of Eden Farm, Southend with his Holstein Champion at the Kintyre Agricultural Society Livestock Show in August, 1983.

The following year Hugh's father Dan McCorkindale who was president of the Autumn Show, won the class for root vegetables with this massive Pentland Hawk potato weighing 4lb 4oz!

Archie Cameron of High Machrimore Farm harvests his last crop of turnips in 1988.

Neil Ronald 'Crocken' and Archie McCallum at the 1988 ploughing competition.

Ploughing Match at Keprigan Farm in 1988. This has been a yearly event for 120 years. Only 12-15 entrants compete now but once there were 104 pairs of horses in a competition.

School Photographs

Pupils and Staff in 1986 Back row L–R: Peggy McCallum (cook), Jen Ronald (ass. cook), David Millan, Andrew Ronald, Peter McVicar, Heather Ronald, Margaret McCallum, Robert Millar, Alec Souden, Kenneth Campbell, Mrs Anderson (secretary),Una Baker (junior teacher) and David Dunbar (head teacher). Middle row: William Hook, ? McKerral, Robbie Glen, Callum Semple, Mark Nelson, Murray Campbell, Justin O'Brien, Stewart Campbell, John NcCorkindale, James Hook, John Ronald, Adrian O'Brien, David Rae and John McTaggart. Front row: Jenny McTaggart, Helen Miller, Rachel Anderson, Isla, Ronald, Laura Watson, Robert Millar, Mairi McFarlane, Mairi McCorkindale, Elaine Hook and Beth Eynon.

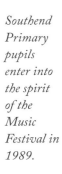

Southend Primary pupils enter into the spirit of the Music Festival in 1989.

Dunaverty Golf Club Celebrates its Centenary

On 19 March, 1989 the Dunaverty Golf Club marked its 100th birthday and the members celebrated with style.

The Golf Club's Centenary Committee.
Back row L-R: N. McConnachie, Robert Millar, Hugh McCorkindale, Dunnie Watson and N. McCallum. Seated: M. McIntyre, Jane McCorkindale, Elsie McKinlay and Jill Middleton.

Toasting the new Dunaverty Golf Club flag are L-R: Robert Millar, Kate McKerral, Belle Robertson, Donny McKerral and Hugh McCorkindale.

The Club's Centenary Dinner was held in April 1989. The top table guests were L-R: Jimmy Wilson, Marjorie Campbell, Sandy Sinclair, Irene Millar, Mrs. McLaren, Belle Robertson, Robert Millar, Jock MacVicar, Miss Wilson, Betty Sinclair, Bob McLaren and Gordon Campbell.

As part of the Centenary celebration the Dunaverty Golf Club hosted the Argyllshire Championship and on the day the Club had more to celebrate than just its centenary, as club member and Southend coastguard, John MacMillan won the competition and raised the trophy.

Southend's Own Belle of the Golfing World

Belle in her Scottish Ladies Golfing Association blazer.

Isabella Robertson MBE was born at Eden Farm, Southend in 1936, the daughter of Hugh and Isabella McCorkindale and sister of Dan who is two years her senior. To her family and friends in Southend she was simply Belle!

Belle says that from an early age she had to take her part in helping to carry out the work on the farm and there was never an idle moment, from helping out with their six Clydesdale horses to bringing in the turnips for the cows' feed, a job she doesn't remember with pleasure as the turnips always seemed to be wet and icy.

However, Belle does attribute her fitness, concentration and discipline in her work ethic to her life on the farm, especially her task in the dairy which entailed carrying and pouring heavy pitchers of milk holding three or four gallons of milk into a container on the top of a refrigerator.

Whatever time she arrived home after a night out she knew her father would only allow her two wake-up calls before she had to be out of bed and to work in the dairy. This sometimes meant she would change out of her evening wear and into her work clothes before laying on top of the bed for a little 'shut-eye' as she knew she dare not get under the bed clothes because she would never be able to rouse herself when her father called her.

Belle was always an athletic child. She says that in Southend although there were tennis courts at both the Keil and Argyll Arms Hotels they were only for the use of the hotel guests.

In the winter the boys had football and in the summer they would practice and compete in the Highland Games around the area. However, both boys and girls could play golf all the year round. Belle enjoyed playing at her local Dunaverty course and when she was 15 or 16 years she joined Machrihannish Golf Club and took lessons from Hector Thomson, who soon recognised that she had a special talent.

Belle told me that she was a very shy and naïve young girl when she left her farm home to compete in her first British Girls Tournament at West Kilbride, but she eventually took all her touring and playing around the world in her stride.

From 1957 until her retirement in 1987 Belle won numerous amateur golfing titles including the British Championship. She was a record seven times Scottish Ladies Champion and represented Scotland 18 times in home international matches. She was also New Zealand Ladies Champion in 1971.

Between 1960 and 1982 Belle played in four Curtis Cup matches and was the non-playing captain on another two occasions. The highlight of her career was when she was a member of the winning Great Britain and Ireland team in the Curtis Cup in 1986 in the USA.

The young Dan and Belle
McCorkindale at Eden Farm.

As an early competitor Belle brings home her golfing trophies to share her
success with her brother Dan.

Captain of the Curtis Cup Team in San
Francisco in 1974.

British Ladies Champion in Conway, Wales in 1981.

Scottish Ladies Champion in 1986.

Curtis Cup Winners at Prairie Dunes, USA, in 1986.

CHAPTER 10

1990s

Southend School pupils entertain the residents of the Auchinlee Eventide Home

The children Back row L–R: Murray Campbell, John McTaggart, Isla Ronald, Morag McCorkindale, Stuart Campbell, Tom Millar, Craig McInnes, Kathleen Thompson, Mhairi Motherwell, John McCorkindale. Front row: David Swain, Robert Eynon, Ronald McCorkindale, Mairi McCorkindale and Richard McKerral.

Mary McCorkindale who with her sister Teenie MacMillan had taught Scottish dancing in Southend for many years, have a night out with some of their pupils. Back row L-R: Mairi MacBrayne, Louise Wilson, Elspth McAllister, Mary McIntyre, Teenie MacMillan, Isobel Ferguson, Ita McShannon and Mary Semple. Front row: Beth Lafferty, Jean McAllister, Mary McCorkindale, Anna Anderson and Ella McLachlan.

Southend School's Shinty Team in 1991. At the back L-R: John Ronald, Murray Campbell and Callum Semple. In the front: Helen Millar, John McCorkindale, Mairi McCorkindale and Beth Eynon.

When Elsie McConnachie, on the left, and Jane McCorkindale represented the Argyll Federation of the SWRI at a golfing competition at Brora, they defeated 22 other Federations to win the silver plate they are holding in this photograph.

Archie Reid now lives in retirement in Southend village but was a third generation farmer at Keprigan Farm. His grandparents John and Mary-Ann Reid moved to Keprigan Farm in 1898 and Archie's father George and his wife carried on the farm in their lifetime.

In 1949 George joined the Ayrshire Cattle Society and started registering his cattle as pedigree Ayrshires. Archie later took over the farm with enthusiasm for the breed and is very proud that he has records of every animal ever bred on his farm.

In 1971 Archie started showing at the local Ayrshire Breeders Club in Kintyre and continued until his retirement with many successes to his name. Archie still travels the world with the Ayrshire Cattle Breeders Association.

Another interest close to Archie's heart is the ploughing competitions that were held on his farm. He remembers with great affection the horses that were born and bred and worked their fields. He says that although tractors must pass MOTs and need spare parts occasionally, horses had to be carefully looked after every day as they were the only mode of transport for all the heavy work on the farm.

Archie Reid with his highest yielding cow Bluebell 20th in 1993. She produced 10 gallons of milk daily.

Bess 167th (the original Bess was registered in 1949) won three trophies in 1998 for Best Heifer in the Ayrshire Championship, Best of Breed Championship and Best Animal in show bred by an Exhibitor. Archie also took home the cup for the best heifer at the local Ayrshire Breeders Competition that year.

At a competition held at Keprigan Farm in 1992 budding young farmers got involved L-R: Audrey Barr from Clockeil Farm and Lorna and John Ronald from Ormsary Farm showing their pedigree Ayrshire calves. John won the championship for the best calf and his sister Lorna claimed second place.

The Dunaverty Players return to Southend triumphant after winning the British Final of the Scottish Community Drama Association competition with their play 'A Slight Ache'. The final was held at Enniskillen in Northern Ireland in 1993.

The cast and crew being piped off the coach are, back row L-R: John and Cathy Kerr, Ronald Togneri, Dr Geoffrey Horton, Lorraine Milligan and Glenda Horton. In front: David McCallum and Alex Ramsey.

John and Cathy Kerr with Dr Geoffrey Horton of the Dunaverty Players display their wining trophies with the backdrop of Dunaverty Beach.

Cubs, Scouts, Guides and Brownies on parade in Southend on Remembrance Sunday 1993.

Back row L-R: Mairi Cameron, Andrew Galbraith, Andrew Miller, Colin McKerral, Thomas Cameron, Ian Semple, Robert Eynon, Andrew Eynon and Amy Taylor. Front row: Claire Martin, Fiona McNidder, Mhairi McNidder, Emma Reid, Lynsey McIntyre, Claire Ronald and Lorna Ronald.

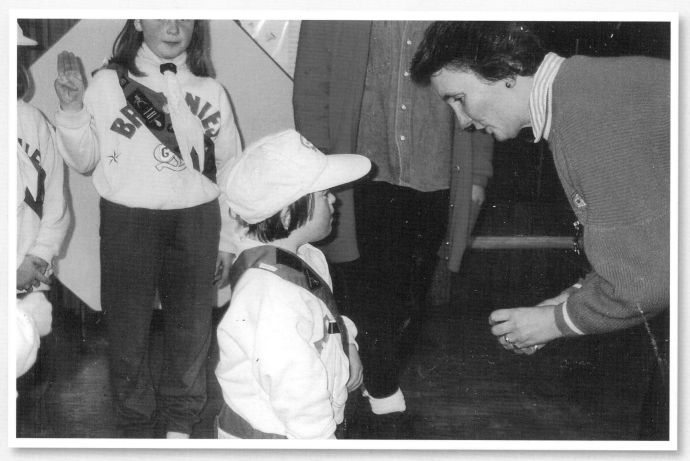

Gillian McIntyre's Brownie Promise Ceremony in 1996.

The Mull of Kintyre – its Lighthouse
and its Keeper Hector Lamont.

The lighthouse sits perched above the savage rocks of the sometimes raging waters of the North Channel that pummel the Mull of Kintyre.

Hector Lamont and his wife Esther were resident at the Mull of Kintyre lighthouse from October 1988 until the light became automatic in March 1996. When I visited them at their home at Stewarton, a mile outside of Campbeltown, they told me that their time at the Mull of Kintyre lighthouse was the happiest they had spent at any of their postings.

Hector had started his career with the Lighthouse Board at Duncansby, John O'Groats, in 1960. After marrying Esther in 1964 they had postings in Orkney, the Isle of Man, the Isle of Tiree, Caithness, Sanda Island and Corsewell Point in Wigtownshire, before moving to this southernmost tip of the Kintyre peninsula.

Esther told me that she thought at first the lighthouse would be too remote for her but she soon came to love it and called it her 'wee heaven', with its goats and other wildlife and the constant procession of shipping and occasional helicopter visit from the Army Signals Corp, who maintained the aerial transmitter near the lighthouse.

Hector told me there were three keepers and a local assistant while they were at the Mull lighthouse and at times their wives would help. Esther laughed as she said there was always something happening. Also they were never without visitors who she loved to entertain, especially their children and grandchildren who came at weekends.

Other visitors ranged from royalty to showbiz stars and from high ranking service personnel to sightseeing holiday visitors, and they were all made equally welcome by this lovely, warm couple.

The hallway in their house bears witness to the high esteem in which they were held by the many branches of the services who gifted them their badges as thanks for the kindness and assistance Hector and Esther gave them during their 'watch' at the Mull of Kintyre lighthouse.

Hector and Esther's grandson Graham Paterson standing next to a vintage Alvis car that was part of a rally that visited the lighthouse in 1992.

Granddaughter Joanne Paterson in the forefront of the picture with a Jaguar XK140 outside the lighthouse. 1992.

Two of the rally entrants admire this 1911 Lorraine Dietrich.

There is no doubt that on a clear summer's day the beautiful wildness of the Mull of Kintyre is boundless and as you travel overland towards the Mull lighthouse the complete serenity and calmness of the area makes you feel you have arrived in God's Kingdom. However, there is another side to this coin when the west wind is howling and the rain lashes down, or when the silent, all enveloping, blinding mists roll in from the sea.

It was an evening like this on 2 June, 1994, when Hector and Esther Lamont were arriving at the top of the hill above the lighthouse after their weekly shopping trip, when overhead they heard the throbbing of a helicopter engine. The next moment the RAF Chinook crashed into the hillside above them and burst into flames with all 29 lives lost. The theories and arguments about this accident still rage on and whatever the cause it has left an indelible scar on all who became involved at the crash site, many of them the Southend auxiliary coastguards.

Without doubt Hector and Esther played their part in the aftermath of this disaster, but like the others they keep their own counsel and the memories run deep. Hector received his MBE from the Queen in 1995 for his service to the Lighthouse Board.

In 1994 as Patron of the Lighthouse Board Princess Anne visited the helicopter crash site and then visited the lighthouse and took refreshments in Hector's House where she signed the visitors' book. (Hector's House is named after one of the first lighthouse keepers. The other house is Harvey's House.)

Hector and Esther Lamont with the photo of them at Hector's investiture at Buckingham Palace.

Hector with his prized memorabilia from his service to the Lighthouse Board – his MBE and the light from the Mull of Kintyre lighthouse, whilst above there is a photograph of the lighthouse.

Southend's Brownies form a guard of honour with lots of smiles and happiness despite lots of rain and wind when Barn Owl Catherine McLean married Douglas Ferguson at St Blaan's Church, in September 1996.

A shooting party at Macharioch Farm
Back row L-R: David Taylor, John Cameron, Barrie Gelder, Neil John McCorkindale, John O'Neill, Gordon ?, John Stewart, Iain McIntyre and Norman O'Neill. Front row: Murdo McLeod, Grant MacPherson, Seamus Kelly, John McCorkindale, Campbell MacBrayne, Patrick Stewart and Scott MacBrayne.

Lorne Cousins, Barrie Gelder, Alistair Cousin, Neil John McCorkindale, John O'Neill, Colin O'Neill, Iain McIntyre and Patrick Stewart.

The 1996 photograph of Southend School pupils

Back row L-R: Head teacher Martin Motherwell, Andrew Martin, Kirsteen McKerral, Louise Anderson, Mhairi McNidder, Archie Ronald, Fiona Bell, Emma Reid, Lynn McCorkindale, Fiona Cameron, Robbie McTaggart and Mrs Lesley Ronald. 2nd row: Mrs Baker, Nicola McConnachie, Ailie McCorkindale, Andrew Galbraith, Catherine Ronald, Craig Galbraith, David Galbraith, Alan Glen, Stephen McKerral, Lorna Ronald, Scott MacBrayne, Julie Galbraith, Christopher Rankin and Mrs Nicholson. 3rd row: Susan Houston, Ashleigh McLean, Jennifer Galbraith, Gillian McIntyre, Ailie MacBrayne, Laura McLean, Alison Semple, Rona MacBrayne, Kirsty Martin, Rebecca McGuire and Becky McTaggart. Front row: Fraser Cameron, Alistair McConnachie, Jamie Ronald, Iain Galbraith, Raymond Morrison, Peter McKerral, Kevin McIntyre and Kenneth Galbraith.

The Rev. Callum O'Donnell takes his horse Jimmy to visit the school children soon after his arrival as Southend's new Parish Church minister.

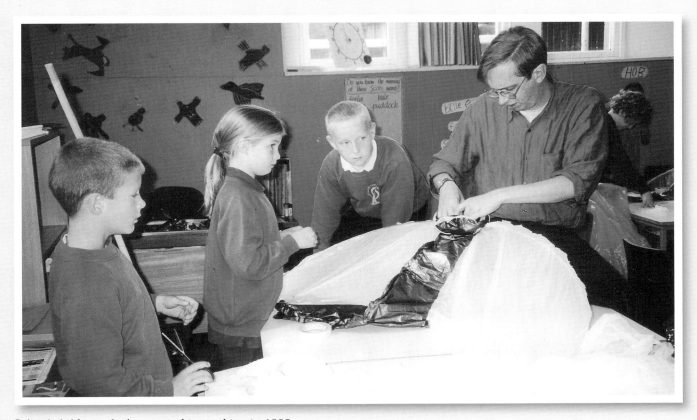

School children take lessons in kite-making in 1999.

When Linda and Bill Brannigan got married on 9 May, 1998, they had the first part of the ceremony at St Columba's footprints with Linda's daughter Alison and son Andrew in attendance.

Their marriage vows were taken at Dunaverty Hall and their reception followed on. This was the first time a marriage service had been held in the hall.

Sybil Kelly and her sister-in-law Margaret Taylor who were two of the original members of the Southend SWRI celebrate the group's 80th year in 1998.

CHAPTER 11

2000

The new millennium celebrated by Southend children in Campbeltown in the summer of 2000.

Southend's G.P. Dr Robert Martin leaves for pastures new in 2001. A farewell party was held at the Muneroy Tea rooms – Dr Robert Martin is in the centre, and his wife Lorna on the left of the picture, with the Chair of Southend Community Council Susan Paterson on the right.

On 28 July 2001 George MacMillan claimed his place in the history of Dunaverty Golf Club when he became the course record holder with a score of 58. It should also be noted that George has been the club champion a record 13 times.

A mural of Dunaverty Rock and Beach painted on one of the school buildings is admired. Standing: Mathew Hales and Jennifer Galbraith. Back row L-R: Becky McTaggart, Susan Houston, Aidan Thomson, Eilidh McLaughlin, Kenneth Galbraith, Fraser Cameron and Craig McKerral. Front row: Karen Semple, Kerri McCorkindale and Ryan Smith.

Julia Knowles moved to the Mull of Kintyre from Kent, with her husband Alan mid-1994. Before long, Julia became Southend's district nurse and says for 10 years she had the privilege to be welcomed not only into the homes of the community, but also into their lives. She also said that the experiences she shared with Southend people – from the beginnings of life until the end of it – will always be her most treasured memories. Recently retired, Julia enjoys life with Alan in their hideaway cottage in the village.

The Dunaverty Players celebrate their Golden Jubilee in 2002. Jill Middleton and John Barbour are seen here cutting the cake.

Southend School pupils, Natalie Smith, Carlyn MacMillan, Stuart McConnachie and Calum Houston, by the Kintyre Information Board at Carskiey Beach.

A reunion was held in 2003 of the staff who worked at the Argyll Arms Hotel in 1963.

Back row L-R: Joanne McPherson, Jennifer Mack, May Barbour, Mamie Robin, Helen Ronaldson, Ann McKinver and Eve Taylor.

Front row: Peggy McCallum, Isobel McPherson, Moira Paterson and Cissie Muir.

Burns Day celebrated at Southend School in 2002

The school cook Peggy McCallum watches over the proceedings as Alistair McConnachie and Jamie Ronald address the Haggis which is piped in by Scott MacBrayne.

Derelict Keil Hotel

In the early 1970s the holiday business was revolutionised when all-in package holidays abroad became accessible to everyone. Hotels that specialized in holiday-makers who returned year upon year soon began to experience an economic down-turn. The Mull of Kintyre was not immune to this change and the Keil Hotel had a regular change of ownership until it closed its doors for the last time in the 1990s. However, there were still the self-catering tourists who came to their caravans sited along the coastline of Kintyre.

Lorna and Andrew Black enjoy an open air meal with their grandmother Sylvia Gilmour at Machribeg Caravan Park at Dunaverty Beach in 2004.

In 2005 these budding builders watch as Southend School's new extension is started.

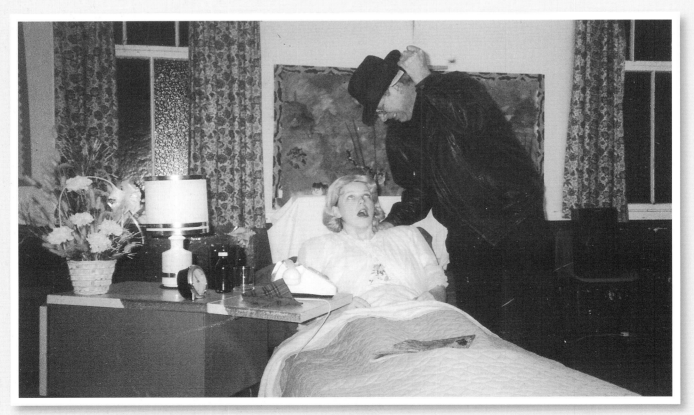

The Dunaverty Players 2005 production was 'Sorry Wrong Number'. Mrs Stevenson, played by Catherine Ann MacVicar, appears to be coming to a sticky end at the hand of George who was played by John Bakes.

2007

Under the tutorage of Ian McKerral, pipers Colin Ronald, Rory McLean, Craig Galbraith, Graeme McConnachie and Stuart MacBrayne, practice in Southend School playground.

Nicola Anderson, Erin McSporran and Katherine Howell enter the dancing competition at the Southend Highland Games in 2007.

**Southend Parish Church Kirk Session
29 April, 2007**

Back row L-R: William McKinnon, Neil Ronald, Malcolm Ronald, James Barbour, John Cameron, William McLean, Thomas Cameron, John Docherty, Alex Ronald and the minister, Martin Forrest.
Front row: Jen Campbell, Jane McCorkindale, Julia Knowles, Elsie McConnachie and Alison Eynon.

Certificates awarded for their long service to Southend's Parish Church were presented by Rev. Martin Forrest to:

William McLean

Alex Ronald.

Clearing the children's play-park in 2007 of its old equipment in order to raise money for an up-to-date 21st century design.
Back row L-R: John Dreghorn, John Bakes, Eleanor McPherson, David McCallum and Janet Ferguson. Front row: Jeanette Dreghorn, Susan Paterson and Donald McPherson.

Whilst many parts of the United Kingdom were awash with flood water in July 2007 the Mull of Kintyre was bathed in tropical sunshine as seen here on Macharioch Beach.

Stones on beach

Jack, Ben and Sam Stone, who were visiting their grandparents, enjoy the Dunaverty Beach waves.

Everyone Enjoys the Southend Highland Games in 2007

Good weather brought crowds of people to watch the dancing competitions.

Visitors are always welcome to join in the fun here. Georgina Martin and her daughter India take part in the mother and child race.

The children enjoy the pony and wagon rides around the sports field.

The Sack Race is taken very seriously by these young entrants.

2008

In April 2008 the Celtic Malts Rally visited the Mull of Kintyre. This E-type Jaguar is seen climbing up Blasthill, before making its way around the Learside Road back into Campbeltown.

The participants of the Conventicle at St Columba's footprints in May, 2008. L-R: Mrs Agnes Stewart (Church of Scotland Reader), Canon Keith Pagan (Retired priest of the Scottish Episcopal Church), Rev. Martin Forrest (Southend's Church of Scotland minister), Rev. Philip Burroughs (minister of the Lorne and Lowland Church, Campbeltown) and Rev. Gary McIntyre (Stirling).

The Pelvic Instability Network Scotland Charity has a fund raising stall at the Highland Games in 2008. The three Trustees of the Charity are behind the stall, L-R: Lesley Murray, Moira Finlayson and Avril Stone.

Daniel and Jean Black as seen in Chapter 8 still return to their caravan at Dunaverty Beach which they have visited for 40 years. Here they are with their family and friends. Back row L-R: Daniel Black, Marie Campbell, Jean Black, Catherine and Robert Black.
Sitting in front are: Ross Knight, Lorna Black and Lynne Campbell.

After a freak August downpour Dunglass Bridge is washed away.

Below: The residents affected by the closure of the road which entailed a long detour on every journey, have a site meeting to discuss the plans of the Argyll and Bute Council to shut the road for 18 months.

L-R: Bruce McConnachie, Catriona McLeod, Robert Miller, Isobel McConnachie, Moira and Charles Finlayson, Hugh Galbraith, Avril Stone, Councillor Rory Colville, Alan Reid M.P., Terry Smith, Neil John McCorkindale, John Murray, Leonard Stokes, Eric Stone and Chairman of the Southend Community Council Susan Paterson.

The new bridge being lowered into place four months later on 23 December, 2008.

The yearly competition of short mat bowls is played at St Blaan's Hall in November 2008.

John Bakes presents the trophy to the winner of the bowls competition Alan Gerrard.

Sybil Kelly's Memories of her Life in Southend

In 2003 I visited Sybil at her home at Macharioch House to chat about her life. I had known her for about 18 months and always found her bright, vibrant and very interesting to talk to, so was more than pleased when she agreed to tell me her life story. Here I share with you some of those memories as many of the facts have already been documented earlier in this book.

Family

Sybil's father was James Taylor, known as Captain Taylor to distinguish him from his son Hamish who was a Colonel, both having served with the Argyll and Sutherland Highlanders. James was born in 1872 at the Argyll Arms Hotel which was owned by his parents. He was the youngest of four with a brother, John, and sisters Mary and Agnes.

After the eldest sister Mrs Mary Gibson was widowed she returned to run the hotel and enterprisingly added a taxi service with horses and carts of all sizes. They also ran a daily service to Campbeltown, with a four horse brake leaving at 10am from Southend and returning from the town at 3pm. It was a popular trip with housewives on market days, Monday.

Sybil's real name was Sibella, after her mother who was the eldest of the 12 Barbour children of Aucharua Farm. Sybil told me that her grandfather John Barbour's family were Ayrshire farmers who had bought the farm and sent him to Southend to run it for them.

Captain Taylor and his wife Sibella farmed at Low Machrimore and had five children – Margaret, a teacher, who married Jim Hunter, a tobacco farmer in Rhodesia but originally from Southend, and who came back to teach at Southend School in her later life; Jean, a doctor, who also finally returned to her Scottish roots, and lived with Sybil and Charlie at Macharioch House; Hamish, who took over the farm from his father; Sybil herself and Mary – the two youngest – who stayed at home and worked with their parents on the farm until the mid 1940s when they took over the Keil Hotel which their father had originally built for them.

Farming

Sybil compared farming today to when she was a child at Machrimore. They had a milking herd but there were no milking machines, so two women from the village came in to do the milking – Rosie McKay and Jane Wilson – and the ploughman's wife would also help. The ploughman Archie MacMillan and his wife lived in a cottage on the farm with their son also named Archie but referred to as 'Erchie'.

There were two maids on the farm. One was the 'outside lass' who did the work around the byre, and the other worked in the farmhouse kitchen and did the housework. When the children were small there was also a nursemaid. Sybil added that her mother made all the butter and cheese which was then sold. Sybil said when she was young farms had people working everywhere but often today there was only the farmer working alone as even his wife usually had a job away from the farm.

She also said that when she was working on the farm or even in the Keil Hotel she rarely had a day off and never a holiday. It was only in the winter that with Mary she would go to Glasgow on the steamer which left Campbeltown Pier at 7.45am and arrived in Glasgow at 1pm. On these trips they would be given money to spend and enjoyed going round the shops where she would buy perhaps a new coat and shoes, or a summer costume or evening dress to wear for the next two years. She said wistfully that everything seemed to have to last two years.

The Territorial Army

Sybil had clear memories of the day her father, Captain Taylor went away to WWI. It was a wet morning of the 6th August, 1914 and the men of the Territorial Army from Southend left in a four horse brake to travel to Dunoon.

They had assembled in the village hall and went on to collect the Captain at Low Machrimore Farm. They were wet through because they had no greatcoats.

Her father sent all the family back to the farmhouse to collect all his coats. She explained that the captain had run the horse business at the hotel before going to the farm so had many large coats – 'Inverness Capes' – and these were soon spread over the shoulders of the men.

The Doctor

Dr Niven spent all his working life in the Parish of Southend. He did not have a surgery as such as he visited his patients on foot, but if he had any distance to travel a car from the Argyll Arms would take him. Dr Niven was also the dentist and Sybil remembers her sister Mary having her tooth 'pulled' by the doctor. She also told me there were no midwives in those days and it was only if the women in the family could not manage that the doctor was called to attend the birth.

After Sybil married Charlie Kelly he managed the bars in the Keil Hotel and, with her sister Mary, they ran the residential side of the business. She said it was a happy hotel where families would return every year for the same fortnight or three weeks. One family always came the last week in July and the first in August, and the only year they missed was when they had twins in the last week of July!

The hotel also hosted weddings and large dances and balls such as the Territorial Ball and these were well supported by people from all around Kintyre.

I asked Sybil what memories she had of Ina Dowager Duchess of Argyll, who once lived at Macharioch House. Sybil said she was "a nice old lady" who rode in a chocolate brown car with the Argyll Coat of Arms painted in gold on the door and with a chauffeur and footman in matching chocolate brown uniforms. The Duchess would call on Captain Taylor when she had business concerning something or someone in the village and he acted as a 'go between'.

The car would pull up at the farm gate and the footman would walk up to the house to see if her father was in. He would then go back to the car and escort the Duchess with her large white chow dog on its lead to the house, and while she was about her business her dog would be walked up and down the lawn by the footman.

Motor Cars

The first motorised vehicle to arrive in Southend was an Argyll motor car in 1903. It was driven by John McNeill, a Glasgow businessman, who drove his father from Glasgow to Southend on the old road. Sybil did not know how long the journey took but she remembered John telling her that the corner at the top of 'Rest and Be Thankful' was so sharp an angle that it took him two attempts to get round it. (Of course this is not the road we use today but the one that comes up from the floor of the valley). John said that after they had completed the manoeuvre he stopped, and when his father asked him why he replied that it was to offer up a prayer that the car had made it that far!

There were no motorised vehicles in this area at that time and therefore no petrol, so it had to be sent on the steamer each day from Glasgow for the duration of the car's visit. Sybil said that most people, goods and mail would travel between Glasgow and Campbeltown by steamer.

Charles Hunter of Machribeg

Macharioch House when Sybil and Charlie moved there in the 1970s.

Farm was the first owner of an automobile in Southend. When Captain Taylor returned from WWI in 1919 he brought with him a Morris car. The first time Sybil travelled to Glasgow by car was in 1920s when she went to one of her sister's graduations with her father.

After selling the Keil Hotel Sybil and Charlie lived at Macharioch House until they died in January 2007, only two weeks apart. It seems appropriate, therefore to write her memories near the end of the book as she made her first appearance near the beginning of it.

CHAPTER 12

Life in Southend 2009

Frances and Ian Hill behind the counter of the Muneroy Stores. Frances has a well deserved reputation for her cooking which keeps the tearooms busy all year round.

The staff of the Medical Practice in Teapot Lane, who look after the health of the Mull of Kintyre residents are – Standing L-R: Trainee doctor Alison Reid, who was on a month's placement before taking her final exams, receptionist Catriona Soudan, Practice Nurse Kitty Millar, Dr James Finlayson, Practice Nurse Fiona McPhee and Receptionist Margaret Bakes. Sitting: Practice Manager Annie Colville and receptionist Mary McKinnon.

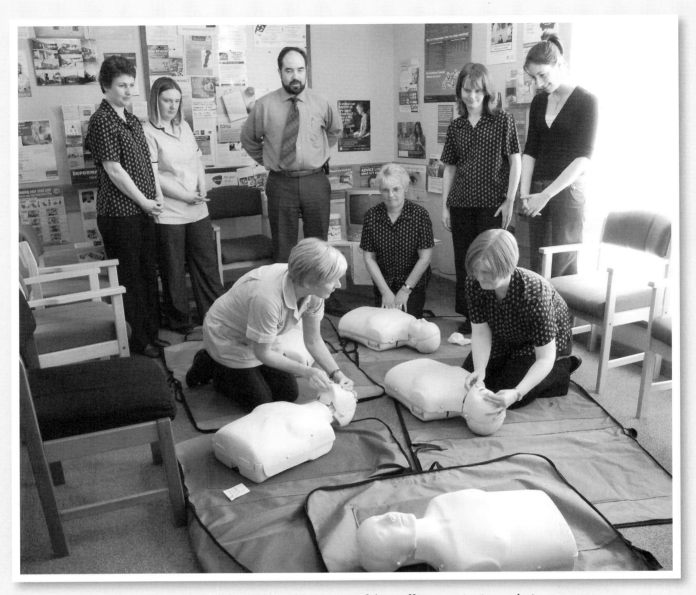

Nurse Fiona McPhee kneeling on the left, up-dates the training of the staff in resuscitation techniques.

Rev. Martin Forrest baptizes Christopher Malcolm Sherwood McEachran at Southend Parish Church on 5 April, 2009.

Kevin McIntyre serving early morning breakfast to his cattle.

The Wednesday Club who meet in the lounge of the hotel every week to enjoy afternoon tea and a friendly chat with the occasional game of bingo for good measure. Around the table from the left are: Margaret Easterbrook, Emily Davidson, Martha Cameron, Mary Galbraith, Margaret and William Robertson.

Southend's own smiling Postie, Joanne Reid, best known to everyone as Joey.

The Argyll Arms Hotel is a well known meeting point for many people as it is not only a residential hotel but also serves meals all day, is an internet café and four mornings a week is also Southend's Post Office!

Mine hosts of the Argyll Arms Hotel, Bill and Margaret Penman, behind the counter of the Lounge Bar.

Post Master Bill Penman exchanges the bar counter for the Post Office counter from Monday to Thursday 10am until 1pm.

Southend Parish Church Guild's 2009 summer outing to Stonefield Castle at Tarbert. Back row L-R: Margaret Russell, Janet Ferguson, Doris Bateman, Elsie Ronald, Christine Ropper, Jean Ronald, Elizabeth Semple and May Barbour. Front row: Susan Cameron, Susan Allan and Margaret Armour.

The Church of Scotland Guild was founded in 1887 by Dr Archibald Hamilton Charteris and the Southend Guild was founded in 1905. The first President was Her Grace, The Dowager Duchess of Argyll who was then living at Macharioch House. There were 45 members in that first year and this year they have 24 members who will be celebrating the 105th anniversary of the Southend Guild.

Their President Margaret Russell told me that the Guild today is about invitation, encouragement, commitment and fellowship which, leads to providing opportunities for continuing growth in Christian faith through worship, prayer and action.

Southend born and bred Wilma McCormick, who now lives in Campbeltown, returns to the village every Wednesday with her mobile fresh fish delivery van.

The Barbour Family of Aucharua Farm in 2009. On the right of the picture is David Barbour, the fourth generation to farm at Aucharua, in front is his son Ruari, David's mother May who with her husband John were the previous generation to farm at Aucharua is in the middle whilst on the left is David's wife Elizabeth and their daughter Emma.

William MacMillan has been the green-keeper at the Dunaverty Golf Course for 34 years as was his father for 22 years before that. William's assistant green-keeper David Scullion is driving the tractor.

Campbeltown Vet Alistair Cousins attends a damaged calf's foot at Macharioch Farm. Alistair, who married Southend headteacher's daughter Ann McLeod in 1970, has tended animals great and small in this area of Kintyre ever since, and is now looking forward to his retirement.

Doris and George Bateman take an afternoon trot with their Welsh mountain pony Champ.

From her home on the Mull of Kintyre Dr. Moira Finlayson updates the PINS (Pelvic Instability Network Scotland) website which she created to help people with pelvic girdle pain. Since setting up the charity 18 months ago Moira has received requests for help from all over the world.

Southend's young footballers

Back row L-R: Donald McPherson, Mark McKinnon, Murray Barbour, Jamie McLean and Jack Galbraith. Front row: Andrew Finlayson, James Baird, Beth Ronald and John McKinnon.

Many of Southend's community gather in June 2009 to wish the Reverend Martin Forrest, his wife Janice and daughter Rachel, farewell as they head off for a new life in Glasgow.